Advance Praise

New entrepreneur? Don't reinvent the wheel! This book is a blueprint for questions, concerns and most of all HELP for *Your First Year*.

— **Karen Campbell**
Campbell's Scottish Terriers

This book is full of cautionary and inspiring tales by women who have been there first and want to make sure you learn from their mistakes. It touches on serious topics, but in a "sure, you can pick my brain over coffee" way.

I love that the first section in the book is on mindset, as too many people discount this step. There are several chapters, so you get exposure to more than one approach.

Throughout the book, each chapter is followed by takeaways, short prompts or exercises that will help you to evaluate your own situation. Which means that reading the book will help you think more clearly about your business!

I've been given a review copy and have already gotten value from just a short read.

—**Julia Poger,** member of AIIC Conference
Interpreter in English, Russian, and French

Every question you would ever have about starting and growing your own business...ANSWERED! How refreshing to have at my fingertips, real stories, and real ideas, in a clean, easy-to-read manner. You can feel the authors' emotions as you read about their experiences and have faith that their suggestions are from tried-and-true circumstances, along with fact-based research. The cherry on top...the key takeaways. Love this!! Thank you for summarizing each section with the spot-on ideas that I can utilize as I develop and grow my own business. *Your First Year: What I Wish I'd Known* is a must have for anyone creating a foundational business!

— **Becca Probst,** author and owner,
Much Love, Becca, transformational coaching
services, soul discovery sessions, and mediumship
healing

What sets *Your First Year: What I Wish I'd Known* apart from other books about entrepreneurship is that it doesn't just provide users with theoretical knowledge; the authors go one step further by including practical tips throughout which make it easier for readers to take actionable steps towards success. This book is perfect for any woman who wants to start her own business but isn't sure where or how to begin; offering real-world advice backed up by evidence makes it easier for women entrepreneurs to make informed decisions in order to reach their goals faster. Whether you're just getting started or you've been running your own business for some time now—this book will help you stay productive while maintaining your mental wellbeing.

— **Dona Rutowicz**, CEO and Founder,
Divorcing Gracefully and Beyond

Where was this book when I started my business? Such a wonderful resource, filled with valuable information, on all facets of entrepreneurship and running a business. I particularly love that each chapter is summarized with "Key Takeaways." Brava to the women authors who shared their own experiences and expertise in this book. It's certain to benefit many entrepreneurs looking to propel their own vision into a real-life business.

— **Susan Shelton**, Wellness consultant and
USANA Independent Associate

Your First Year: What I Wish I'd Known offers sage advice to women who are preparing to step into the business world! Each chapter offers clear steps to take to create a healthy support network. The personal narrative is relatable and offers support to the reader who may be experiencing overwhelm and lack of confidence about taking those first steps.

— **Amy Bond Taliaferro**, Integrative Bodywork

If you're considering starting a business or navigating your first years, this book is for you. Compassion, encouragement and practical information intersect in *Your First Year*, as women share their own experience, knowledge, and strategies learned through starting and establishing their businesses. You'll find something of value in each chapter to support you on your business journey!

— **Becca Weinstein**, Intuitive visionary, energy
coach, and artist,
InnerFire Visioning for Empowered Alignment

I was fortunate enough to review an advanced copy of *Your First Year*. This collection of essays offers some solid business advice for both new and seasoned entrepreneurs. The stories shared by the contributors are relatable and entertaining. The brevity of the essays allows the reader to enjoy a few entries at a time and be able to fully process each one.

— **Melissa Mitchel Willis** Coach, consultant, and speaker

Success leaves clues and *Your First Year* provides a plethora of personal wisdom, insights, advice, and inspiration that will help you move through your first year of business with confidence and know-how. This is the book that many seasoned entrepreneurs wish they had when starting out. If you want to start off strong in your first year of business, then this book is a must read.

— **Kendra Woods, MBA**, CEO + Founder of The Prosperous Projector

Your First Year

Your First Year

What I Wish I'd Known

Edited by
Deborah Kevin & Jill Celeste

HIGHLANDER
PRESS

ISBN: 978-1-956442-11-3
Ebook ISBN: 978-1-956442-12-0
Library of Congress Control Number: Applied For.

Published by Highlander Press
501 W. University Pkwy, Ste. B2
Baltimore, MD 21210

Cover design: Hanne Brøter
Managing Editor: Deborah Kevin, MA
Associate Editor: Jill Celeste, MA

For every little girl who dreamed of being her own boss,
and for every woman who became her own boss.

Contents

Introduction
Deborah Kevin, MA

When *Your First Year* was first conceived, the women I spoke with about sharing their business start-up experience with others responded with a wholehearted and collective, "Yes!" It's this kind of generosity of spirit and wisdom that reminds me how important it is to give women a voice, to allow them to share from their hearts, and provide a platform to make their wisdom available to those who desperately need it.

When I left the corporate world in 2010, I never dreamed that I'd own a business, one that morphed over time to allow me to serve writers and authors in a way that I couldn't comprehend back then. My first business began by accident, born from a request to design and create a website. Then more requests came in. I tapped into my "can do" attitude, learned, and put into practice what came to me. I also made a lot of mistakes. A LOT of mistakes. Shame snuck into my consciousness. As a former accountant, who held a change leadership certification from Cornell University and a Six Sigma Black Belt, I thought I *should* know how to run a business.

Every piece of advice I heard, I followed. This resulted in chaotic vibrations—and not much forward momentum. Eventually, I stopped *shoulding* on myself and embraced my natural skillset. I focused on what I naturally loved to do (hint: it had to do with books, a love affair that began when I was four), and magic happened. I learned to trust myself, to listen to my gut (or intuition), and leaned into my gifts. I learned how to discern what would work for me and my clients—my ideal clients. I also learned how to say, "No."

That's when magic happened.

The book you hold in your hands contains hard-earned wisdom, shared from a place of love and encouragement. Consider it written for you because we have your back and want you to make a positive impact in our world. We believe in you!

So, whether you're a seasoned entrepreneur or a woman contemplating your place in the gig economy, you will find exactly what you need within these pages.

Together, we can change the world.

Deborah Kevin, MA
Chief Inspiration Officer
Highlander Press

Part One
MINDSET

Focus, Faith, and Friendship

Suzanne Tregenza Moore

TEXT EXCHANGE:

Me: I just got fired.

Amara: Are you okay?

Me: I would do a cartwheel out the glass doors if I didn't think I would cause myself physical harm in the process.

I'D FELT IT COMING. FOR WEEKS, EVERY TIME I ENTERED THE office the hairs stood up on the back of my neck and I braced for impact. Many of those who'd reported to the former CEO were shown the door. It was only a matter of time.

Two years earlier, I'd intended to give my notice, but September 2008, when the real estate bubble burst and banks went out of business, turned out to be a time that quitting a solid job seemed foolish. So, I stayed through the birth of my second son and instead shifted to part-time.

Emotionally though, I was done with that job. I'd learned what I believed I could learn, and it was time to move on.

I packed up a small box of personal items—the sticky note

pictures drawn by my former boss, the blue and white pottery mug which held my pens and pencils made for me by a dear friend, and the ribbon board that held pictures and invitations which had been meaningful to me throughout my tenure at the company. I closed up the box, exited through the glass doors, went down in the elevator, and out to my car.

It was time to start my own business.

Before the birth of my older son, I'd served clients as a health coach at night while working my full-time corporate job. The busier I became as a mom—first with one son, then with two—the more my side gig got lost in the shuffle. In my heart, I knew I was meant to work for myself, but my tantalizing steady paycheck at an MBA level salary kept me showing up.

Being let go from Cinedigm gave me the opportunity to focus on my own business. Unfortunately, I did anything but focus.

I quickly found myself panicking about my lack of income. I'd made good money at my corporate job and felt a lot of pressure to backfill my salary. Friends and acquaintances shared the many things they did to supplement their health coaching incomes: selling essential oils, vitamins, skin care, and exercise systems. I got lost in the shuffle.

I tried too many solutions. Invested in the starter kit of too many product lines.

Six months after I lost my job, I'd also lost my way. I had no clear message, no clear client base, and was trying to sell too many things.

It wasn't until I attended my first entrepreneurial conference that I realized two things:

1. I was going in too many directions, and
2. I was not using my greatest gifts.

I desperately needed to focus, and I needed to do focus on what I discovered was my unique brilliance: technology came easily to me. I left the conference and decided to make a major shift to something I was uniquely suited for. I started a virtual assistant business.

My husband was puzzled. He didn't understand why I wouldn't do both health coaching and virtual assistance.

I told him with great clarity, "I need to do just one thing. I need to be focused. I need people to know me for this."

This was the beginning of my first bit of entrepreneurial success. I was off and running.

Once I focused and worked in my unique brilliance, I immediately began getting clients. I served them well, got lots of referrals, and was soon bringing on team members.

Within a year, I felt the strain of trading dollars for hours. I tried a lot of new and scary tactics to leverage myself and develop new streams of income.

I jumped into teaching tele-classes, not worrying about whether people would show up to them. I built courses I knew my people needed. I shot videos with an old digital camera—because when I started smartphones were not yet ubiquitous.

Determined not to get hung up on excuses, I tried many avenues for growth. What I didn't realize was how weak my overall confidence was and how that would impact me.

As entrepreneurs, we create an environment for ourselves where we must take risks despite our fears. Often, because we are taking risks, we fail, which confirms our fears.

It can be a vicious circle!

Until we realize that with each "failure" we can learn something. Each failure leads us to success. We just don't know how many failures we need to endure until we get there.

Often, as entrepreneurs—especially during the new, failing forward phase of our businesses—what we cannot see is our own success.

When I look back on my early years in business, I see that faith in myself, my knowledge, and my instincts were what was missing.

Throughout the years, I've watched others succeed with the same courses I tried to sell back then. Truth: when I look at Amy Porter-field's success, I have a small desire to scratch out my own eyeballs.

Back in 2011, she was not far ahead of me in her messaging and success. Now she's making millions and everyone in internet marketing knows her name.

Sadly, I don't have to ask myself why that is. It is not a mystery.

I left opportunities on the table because of a lack of faith in myself. When challenges arose, I didn't tackle them. I turned away from them, assuming I was wrong to have tried whatever it was I'd tried.

In some courses, I enrolled a handful of students the first time I promoted them. Instead of celebrating, I saw outcome as failure.

Instead of reviewing my marketing plans for these programs, increasing my outreach, and trying again, I reinvented the programs themselves, reworking my messaging and confusing the heck out of my community.

I don't know a single entrepreneur who doesn't sometimes speak down about herself— internally and externally. I certainly did during those early years.

And today, I see this behavior in my clients. They often tell me first about what they haven't done, or what they've done wrong, or what hasn't gone well. These admissions come long before telling me about something good.

It is natural for us to discount our successes because they can seem easy and, therefore, unimportant. A human default focuses on what went wrong. Unfortunately, this creates an unseen, but critical barrier, to success.

When you focus on what is going wrong, you invite others to do the same. If you arrive at a meeting sharing the snafus of your day, rather than what is going right, your colleagues, friends, and referral partners are unlikely to hire or refer you believing you are over-whelmed and not ready for more.

Alternatively, if you show up in a state of positivity and faith, sharing what is going well, you will send the message that you are ready for more. Consciously or unconsciously, others will respond in kind.

I'm not suggesting that you sugar coat your experiences, or "fake it 'till you make it." But look for the good in what you've accomplished and share it whenever you are given the opportunity. Most importantly, believe in yourself, in what you are accomplishing, and in what you are learning. Have faith that it will lead you to something bigger.

My success has come in fits and starts. As I look back upon my twelve years as an entrepreneur, I can clearly see that the friendships I developed with other entrepreneurs have created the greatest impact on my success.

Speaking positively about your accomplishments makes others feel positive about you and your business. Having a group of trusted friends who understand what you are experiencing and who are willing to unpack your challenges with you is equally as important.

Save your challenges for the conversations you have with people who are emotionally invested in your success: those who are willing to guide you, share their own challenges, and help you build upon what's going well.

Allowing myself to be vulnerable with entrepreneurs I trust is a choice that has created more value in my business than I could adequately calculate. When I look back at the times that I've cocooned myself from my entrepreneurial communities, I noticed slower growth, more struggle, and less self-confidence.

Conversely, when I look back on the times I've moved through challenges with loving support, the result was growth. There are always challenges because entrepreneurship is, by its nature, pushing through newness. The delta is the surrounding community.

When I'm asked, "What do you want to tell someone who is their first year of entrepreneurship?" My answer is:

- Focus—on what you do best, what comes naturally, and on clarity of your message to others;

- Faith—have it in yourself, your intuition, and your solutions; and
- Friendship—surround yourself with entrepreneurial friends who have your back, believe in you, and remind you of the change maker you are when you feel depleted.

KEY TAKEAWAYS

- How do you evaluate your level of focus in your business? Do you believe that others understand exactly what you offer?
- Can you think of a time when you lost faith in your offering? Was there a set of circumstances that shifted your confidence?
- Do you have a community of entrepreneurs you trust to help you see the best of yourself and what you offer? Are you meeting with them often enough?

Intuition: Key to Your Business Planning

Nicole Meltzer

"THE TIME HAS COME. BEGIN YOUR JOURNEY OF RELEASING your massage therapy practice and dedicate your work entirely to helping others open their intuition. One year from now, you will understand why you needed to begin this process today."

I received this mysterious message in my morning meditation on March 14, 2019. Umm, what? Massage therapy was my main income stream. I had been practicing for two decades, was established in the industry, and had a full client roster. In Ontario, Canada, massage therapy is a regulated health profession. Most extended health insurance plans covered massage, so I didn't need to put on a marketer's hat to fill my practice. Word of mouth led to my full roster, and my clients' insurance coverage ensured a guaranteed minimum number of sessions per client. I could, essentially, forecast my yearly massage therapy income with ease. Safety. Security. This is what my massage therapy practice offered me.

On the other hand, teaching intuition was a different income stream altogether! Although I had been leading intuitive development classes for years, I hadn't put much effort into marketing the classes because I relied on my massage therapy practice as my primary income source. The idea of generating a marketing plan left me less than enthused. Secretly, though, I felt a wave of relief in receiving this message. It was as if I was receiving a permission slip to do the work I genuinely wanted to do; and confirmation that it would be okay. I knew I didn't have another decade of massage therapy left in me. My body was starting to show signs of wear and tear from the decades of massaging, and I wondered if my guides were alluding to a future injury. What would happen in a year?

I live my life paying attention to the whispers of the Universe, which doesn't mean I don't question the guidance when it arrives. These questions are especially true when the guidance significantly impacts income. When that happened, it was easy to let my ego get in the way of understanding the messages. This is a lesson I learned the hard way. Time and again, when the messages were illogical, I dismissed them as fanciful imaginations, only later to find out they were creative solutions showing me a more straightforward path forward on my journey. I now follow a simple process for intuitive guidance, which has proven invaluable to me in business planning, marketing, and life.

The first step in the process is to dream. Daydreaming is one of my favorite activities. I feel free and uninhibited when I'm daydreaming. The more outrageous the dream, the better. It invariably ignites my creative juices and excites me for the planning process. To get my daydreaming started, I imagine myself at a dinner party with friends. It's the end of the year, and we're celebrating everything we've accomplished and experienced throughout the past year. When it's my turn to share, I let my imagination go wild. My editing and logical brain is not allowed to attend this party! From the plethora of scenarios I relay, I pay attention to the ones which really light me up. These are the ideas that I'll take with me into the next step of the intuitive process.

Once I have a list of the ideas, I bring my analytical brain back online. How feasible are these options at this time? What would it take to bring them to fruition? Are they in alignment with my long-term vision for the business? This part of the process usually leaves me with some ideas to implement. I never discard the other ideas entirely because I would never want to toss aside anything that lights me up. If my soul called it forward, there is a reason for it. It just might not be the right time to implement it now. Interestingly enough, I often find that, while working on the other ideas, the ideas on the back burner tend to find a way to manifest anyway!

Now that I have one or two ideas, I again ask for guidance. If the ideas cannot be implemented simultaneously, and I need to focus on only one at a time, I play a version of my "Power of Three" game. First, I give my guides a time parameter, such as "during the next twenty-four hours" or "on my walk in the forest today." Then I allocate an object to each idea. The object is possible to witness as I go about my day but not necessarily probable. For example, if I'm going for a walk in the forest, I wouldn't allocate a squirrel to one of the items because I'm guaranteed to see multiple squirrels during my walk. However, I could say a black squirrel with a white-tipped tail. They exist in my neighborhood's forest, but I don't often see them. With objects allocated to each idea, I then ask my guides to show me, during the time parameter I decided on, three of the objects allocated to the idea which is in my best interest to pursue at this time. Then I go about my day. At the end of the period, I saw what the results were. Sometimes there is one winner. Sometimes there are none. And sometimes there are multiple. If there are multiple winners and I feel like I can't possibly focus on all of them right away, I repeat the process with the question, "What is the best option to begin with?" I've learned to be okay with whatever the result may be. In due time, all options which serve me will step forward.

The next and final step is the one with which I have the most fun. This step is put on repeat until the manifestation process is complete. Any questions about the idea, or now more accurately labeled the intention, or questions about the next action steps to take are addressed in this step. This is when you are in conversation with the Universe. The Universe, Spirit, guides, Higher Self, whichever name you use to describe the energies guiding you along your path, send you messages continuously in the form of metaphor. You receive these metaphors through the senses of the intuitive system—the clairs. You have a primary and secondary clair that you are using all the time, you just may not be aware of it. If you would like to learn more about the clairs, I go into a detailed description of each clair in my book, *Intuitive Languages*.

To give you an idea of how you may be receiving messages now, let's use the example of clairvoyance (seeing) and clairaudience (hearing) as the primary and secondary clairs. Let's say you are driving, and simultaneously you see a sign (like a bumper sticker on the car in front of you) and hear a song on the radio with key phrases which would apply to your intention. You would put those words together to identify your message. Another, more metaphorical example would be seeing a specific animal and hearing the song of a specific bird. In this case, you would ask yourself, "What does a (name of animal) mean to me?" or "What makes an (animal) different from another animal?" Then do the same for the bird. The meaning you attach to the animal and the bird will give you a message. Let's say you saw a rabbit and heard a crow, and your question was about a decision to be made. You have deciphered a rabbit to represent speed and a crow to represent high intelligence. The message would be to be quick and thoughtful about your decision. In other words, this would be a time to tune into your logical side more than your emotional side and to take action quickly. This is a lot of fun to practice, and, with time, you can begin to receive detailed, in-depth messages to help you along your path to manifestation.

After receiving the message on March 14, 2019, I went through this simple process to better understand what guidance was offered. To validate that I had understood the message correctly, I asked to be shown three robins before sundown. I hadn't yet seen robins that spring, so I felt this was a bit of a gamble. I ran some errands, and when I arrived home, three robins were on my driveway, looking at me as I approached. There was no mistaking it: that was my validation! Then I asked about steps in transitioning out of massage therapy into focusing solely on intuitive work. I received a message each day, took action on it, and repeated the same process the next day. My intuitive membership program, Flow, grew at the same pace I released massage therapy clients. It was a smooth and gentle transition.

One year later, on March 14, 2020, Ontario was placed on lockdown. Only essential service workers were allowed to continue working with the public in person. Massage therapy was not deemed essential, leaving thousands of massage therapists without an income. I am so grateful I listened to the guidance.

KEY TAKEAWAYS

- You are intuitive. The Universe is sending you messages daily via metaphors.
- Although your intuitive messages can seem illogical at times, they offer you creative solutions to challenges and, ultimately, a less complicated path forward to your goals.
- Intuition is the secret ingredient of your business planning. The Universe will always show you the gentlest path to your destination. The trick is in trusting what you are shown!

Don't Let Your Subconscious Ruin Your Business!

Nancy Linnerooth

GILLIAN WAS SURE THIS LATEST COACHING PROGRAM WOULD BE different. After all, it promised if she just followed the step-by-step process, she would soon be making $10,000 per month in her business. Its raving fans swore that all they did to take their businesses from nothing to six figures were to follow the steps.

More importantly, Gillian had paid a *huge* amount of money to sign up. If that wasn't enough to get her off the couch and doing what was needed to grow her business, nothing would be. In fact, Gillian had decided that, if this program didn't work, she would give up her dream of having her own business and go back to a corporate job.

In spite of all that, it wasn't working. In three months, Gillian had completed exactly one and a half of the twenty-four modules.

Now Gillian was a smart woman with a master's degree. She knew what she had to do to grow her business. She was capable of completing all the modules. She was extremely motivated to help others with her business—not to mention make back the money she'd invested in the program.

Still, she was stuck.

Tears leaked out of the corners of her eyes as Gillian told me her story over Zoom. She shrugged her shoulders, shook her head, and started telling me things I'd heard from so many business owners.

"I must be lazy."

"I guess I'm not motivated enough."

"Or maybe I'm just a bad businessperson."

Gillian was wrong. It was none of those things. This was not some sort of moral failing. What was holding Gillian back was something in her *subconscious* mind blocking her from the success she *consciously* wanted.

I knew that once we'd identified and released the subconscious blocks in her way, Gillian would be able to get moving on those modules, grow her business, and change her life.

So, we got to work.

Subconscious blocks hold women business owners back in so many ways. They can show up as:

- Keeping busy doing everything except what will make you more money.
- Avoiding something that makes you uncomfortable, like asking for the sale.
- Struggling to make decisions.
- Planning to make videos for a new program and then never recording them. Or not releasing them.
- Getting a scratchy voice—or losing your voice entirely—when making an offer from the stage.
- Delaying hiring help you desperately need, sometimes for years.
- Not raising your rates, even when you know you're undercharging.
- Working way too hard without making any real progress.
- Sabotaging yourself and your business when things start to go well.
- And many, many more.

BOTTOM LINE: IF YOU CAN SEE THE NEXT LEVEL FOR YOUR business but can't seem to get there, you probably have a subconscious block—or more than one—getting in your way.

I created my MVP Activator program to get rid of the common and not-so-common subconscious blocks that hold women entrepreneurs back. I called this program "MVP" because entrepreneurial blocks fall into the three main areas of Mindset, Visibility, and Profitability. *Mindset* includes any block telling you that you don't deserve success or support. *Visibility* covers any block preventing you from getting your message out in a bigger way. And *Profitability* is all things money. Entrepreneurs need to clear these common and less-common MVP blocks, even the ones they don't realize they have, to get to the next level.

WHAT IS A SUBCONSCIOUS BLOCK?

A subconscious block is a rule, belief, or fear you've internalized, often in childhood, that gets triggered when you go after your goal.

Motivation or willpower are not enough to overcome a subconscious block. And no amount of reasoning with yourself will get rid of one either. As far as your subconscious is concerned, that block is keeping you safe, loved, and cared for, which will always win out over your conscious desires.

It's as if you have an old cassette tape playing a message in your mind. No matter how loudly you yell at it, that message won't change. To replace it, you need to hit the <Record> button.

That's what EFT (or "tapping" as I usually call it) can do.

WHAT IS TAPPING?

Tapping is a technique where you tap on points on your body. While tapping on those points, you can "talk back" in different ways to your subconscious and release the block internalized there. It's the best approach I've found to actually get rid of subconscious blocks.

For Gillian, we released a rule that she should not outshine her brother Greg. Their parents doted on Greg when Gillian was growing up, going to all his games and praising everything he did, no matter how trivial.

Meanwhile, nothing Gillian did was ever enough. When she'd tell them about an accomplishment—getting straight A's, being chosen for a choir solo, winning the class spelling bee—her parents would immediately say something about how smart or popular Greg was.

Gillian learned she wasn't supposed to do better than Greg. She internalized that Mindset block early and forgot it by the time she was an adult. Consciously, anyway.

Greg led a normal, average life. Meanwhile, Gillian was on a path to do so much more. She developed an approach she knew would help many families stop fighting *and* make her a lot of money in the process. No wonder her subconscious block kept her from completing the coaching program that promised her success!

With Tapping, we released Gillian's block around Greg in a couple of sessions. As that rule unraveled, she started completing modules.

We weren't done yet, though.

Often a business owner will have more than one subconscious block, and Gillian was no exception. Together we uncovered and released multiple blocks slowing her down.

One of Gillian's biggest Profitability blocks was a money ceiling, which is like a subconscious thermostat that limits the amount of money you can have in your life. Most of us have a money ceiling, although the amount is different for everyone.

Whenever you're in danger of making too much money (whatever that is for you), your money ceiling will cause you to take action, or avoid taking action, so you don't end up with more money than is subconsciously "comfortable."

If you have a big revenue month, your money ceiling might cause you to slow down your marketing so you bring in less for a couple of months. Or it might cause you to get rid of the "excess" money by reinvesting in your business and not paying yourself enough.

Your money ceiling is usually set-in childhood based on what you saw or heard in your family. As an adult, your money ceiling allows you to have the amount of money that makes you feel the same way you did growing up. If your family was always scrambling to pay the bills, you'll recreate that feeling now. Which means, even if you bring in a decent amount of money, you'll find there are always more expenses than income.

Gillian's father had always talked about how they didn't have enough money for any extras. So Gillian's money ceiling wouldn't let her complete the modules that promised she would make so much from her business that she would be able to buy lots of "extras."

With a single session, we raised Gillian's money ceiling. The next week she reached out to three families she had been avoiding. Two signed up for her program on the spot. One mother even hugged her, saying how relieved she was to finally be able to repair her relationship with her son.

Over the course of six months, Gillian and I identified and released numerous subconscious blocks that had been preventing her from moving forward. She completed all the modules in the coaching program. She started speaking to small groups of parents, sending out newsletters, and offering her program to all who expressed an interest. She was making a name for herself in her region as an expert in parenting teens, clients were referring their friends, and the revenues in her business were going up.

All this became easy once she cleared out her subconscious blocks.

It turns out that clearing subconscious blocks is something advancing entrepreneurs do throughout their business journey, no matter how successful they become. Owners of six-figure and seven-figure businesses come to me to grow their businesses to the next level. They've learned that, in order to up-level, the first thing they need to do is get rid of blocks that are triggered and hold them back.

Now you know, too.

Please remember how powerful your subconscious is. It can limit you and your business no matter how motivated and capable you are.

So, if you ever find that you or your business are stuck, change your subconscious. Tapping is a great way to do that.

KEY TAKEAWAYS

- Your *subconscious* mind can block you from the success you *consciously* want by causing you to do things like procrastinate, avoid taking certain actions, or even sabotage your business.
- To up-level and make more money, become more visible, or have a bigger impact, you need to first release subconscious blocks in your way.
- Motivation, willpower and logic are not enough to get rid of subconscious blocks. For that, you need something like Emotional Freedom Techniques (EFT or "Tapping").
- Whenever they are ready to level-up, advancing entrepreneurs clear out their subconscious blocks first, no matter how successful they already are.

Step Up and Own
Your Unique Brilliance
Maribeth Decker

I HESITANTLY STEPPED UP TO THE MICROPHONE, WAITING TO ASK my first question at a mentor training with about 100 attendees. I imagined the participants turning to look at me like some sci-fi horror scene. Was I trembling? You bet! *How short am I? I can't even reach the mic!* I stood on my tiptoes to reach the mic and whispered, "Hi, I'm Maribeth Decker, and I am an animal communicator."

I braced myself to be laughed at, sneered at, and imagined people staring at the crazy lady at the mic.

My mentor spoke. "May I coach you, Maribeth?" she asked with love.

"Yes, that's why I'm here," I said as I wondered if I was about to be criticized or condemned.

She said, "Grab the microphone and bring it down to your mouth, like it's yours, and you own it."

Who am I to be holding a microphone and talking like I'm someone to be listened to? But I followed her guidance.

Next, she asked me to straighten up, look her in the eye, and speak the truth of who I am. "But this time, act as if you own it."

Oh, crap. Really? I have to say this in a loud voice? Say it clearly? I grumbled inwardly. *All I want to do is ask a question, run back to my seat, and cower like a frightened puppy.* I gave myself the fastest pep talk I could muster. *You have to get comfortable with who you are if you're going to connect with your ideal clients. Start now!*

And so, I said as fiercely and clearly as I could manage, "I'm Maribeth Decker and I'm an intuitive animal communicator."

The nod of approval and joy in her face calmed and strengthened me. Then I asked my question.

That was an incredibly crucial moment for me and my business, although I didn't know it at the time. I sat down after stepping down from the mic, unable to look at anyone, waiting for my heart rate to return to normal.

I finally began to grasp this moment's significance when friends shared that they witnessed my transformation in that moment at the microphone. They described watching me come out of my shell, like a turtle who knows she's safe and she's got a clear path—and who knows she's not stopping.

One lovely friend shared that she cried as she saw me embrace and own who I was. I had not yet settled into this "new" but truer understanding of who I am meant to be in this world. But even today, my business supporters continue to remind me of my transformation when I need it.

If you are going to attract clients who are "just right" for you, you must embrace and delight in who you are, your unique "flavor" or skill set among the many other wonderful people with the same title or business. If you're not in love with what you do and how you do it, how will others see your brilliance?

I'm not advocating for a big ego, though. There's a way to be confident about who you are and what you do which doesn't have to extend into "I'm the best." I believe each person offers something special that will be of the best service for each client. You don't have to be everything for everybody. Find those who delight you and craft your message from your heart to get their attention.

And there's an alternate to the *I'm the best*, which is still our ego taking over: *I'm the worst.* Negative thinking can set in when you don't see the results you hoped for. Especially when you work with other souls (usually we say people, but in my business, I work with a lot of different species). Because they have their own personalities, peculiarities and preferences, they may not align with what you hoped would happen.

To continue to believe in myself, I take what I call a spiritual approach. I set the intention that whatever I do is for their highest good. And that what I do is real. Many beings support me. I remind myself that how my work manifests in the 3D world is not up to me. I emanate rapport and compassion as we work together. Even if they have a different path than the one I thought we were on together, I have learned to turn them over to Source. I trust that they have chosen the right path for themselves.

I also ask for testimonials when people tell me that our session with them and their animals went well. The testimonials are on the "Success Stories" page of my website. When doubt sets in, I re-read them to remind myself, "Hey, what you do is real. Lives change for the better! There is more joy and peace in these human-animal relationships!"

Also, having a community that sees your worth and believes in what you do is essential. We need people who share what's working for their business, refer us, and to whom we can refer, and, when warranted, call us on our bull****.

Otherwise, we tend to get into that mindset of "Stinking Thinking," or—this makes me laugh) — "Mental Masturbation." We dig our mental pit deeper and deeper without even realizing it. It's full of assumptions about others' judgements of us and stories we tell ourselves without knowing they're true.

When this occurs, I become less brave. I don't step out when an opportunity presents itself. I start to expect bad outcomes or wonder why the heck I even try.

But with the support of others, I see the opportunity of connecting with more people and pets. I experience joy and excitement in addition to the jitters. And when things don't go as planned, friends remind me to look for the lesson. Get back up, clean myself off, and move on. That is life affirming. Because, at some point, we're all going to bomb.

Another way I own my brilliance is by speaking and writing clearly and consistently about my accomplishments. This is another area where I needed help from people who knew my worth. They reminded me about accomplishments I'd forgotten or didn't think were big deals. If my peers think something was a big deal, it was probably a big deal to others. For instance, I'm an Amazon bestselling author. My goal is to say and write it that way consistently. I shifted from saying I'm the "author of the bestselling book" to "I'm a bestselling author." I'm super uncomfortable with that change, but it's more powerful and true.

How can you craft your words to speak and write the truth about your worth? List your accomplishments first and ask your supportive peers what they might add. Work with someone who works magic with words, if that's not your strong suit. Practice speaking your accomplishments out loud, first by yourself if necessary. Then use them in your introduction, on your website, in your bio, and on social media.

At some point, you need to *own mastery of your craft*. By this I mean, you've stopped taking courses just to make sure you're good enough. Yes, you still take courses, but you've shifted your mindset. You're no longer the perpetual student who hasn't gotten enough credentials to feel like the real deal. Instead, you're the master practitioner, honing your abilities and skills to help more people. Can you feel the different energy in those perspectives? The student mindset looks outward for approval, for that passing grade. It decreases our trust in ourselves, in our sense of resilience. The master practitioner creates a few new twists on what they learned or re-engineered the information for their particular clients.

I surely didn't feel like the master in my first year of business. Truthfully, I'm just now owning my leadership. From experience, I ask you to hold the intention or goal that you're going to become a master of your craft. This is not a Big Ego mindset. In reality, it comes from a place of feeling grounded with support from beings in this world and the next. Have faith in what you do. When you get off track or make a mistake, you own up, fix it, and get back on track. Maybe you'll get more training or feedback to do better the next time. But you don't stay in blame and victimhood. Never give up! Stay grounded in the truth that you and only you can bring this unique "something" to this planet.

In all transparency, I'm writing this for myself as much as for you, my friend. "Stepping into my unique brilliance" has been and continues to be my biggest challenge. But it has also been the biggest opportunity to grow into my "best self." The one I sometime glimpse and others see for me. Step into your best self! I believe in you!

Key Takeaways

- You are brilliant. Trust yourself and lean into your true purpose knowing you are supported.
- Even if what you want to do seems incongruent with what you've done in the past, trust that what you want is truly important and valuable.
- Your ego's job is to keep you safe—but you can't grow as you're intended if you listen to it all the time. Trust your gut, and tell your ego, "Thank you. I'm safe, and I've got this."

Boundaries for Success

Jennifer Kate

"HOW DID I GET HERE...?" I SAID TO MYSELF, AS I SAT QUIETLY, staring past the calendar showing on the screen of my iMac. It was only 1:30 pm and I was already running on empty. I hadn't had lunch yet, still had a full day of client calls, school pick-up, dinner duty, a teacher conference, and I had no idea how I was going to make time to work on the client project that was due for my meeting the next day. How could I muster up the energy to do all of those tasks when my body screamed at me to take a break? I put my face in my hands. *"This is chaos,"* said my inner voice. *Why am I even doing this? My nine-to-five was SO much easier. This isn't even worth it!"*

We don't expect to feel this way or experience so much stress when we begin our businesses, but it can be a reality for many women after their first year or two on their entrepreneurial journey. In just three years, my client Emily had gone from a passion-filled woman, on a mission to build a business that will impact the world, to feeling completely burned out and disconnected, so desperate for rest and time with her family, that she would walk away from what she once felt was her 'calling' to go back to her cubicle.

Entrepreneurs often start their businesses with a mission in mind.

They may be working towards impacting the lives of others or achieving a place of freedom to so live a life they love, a life that gives them the space to spend more time with their families, to play, and travel, etc. They are driven to achieve what they set out to do and have the mindset that makes them unstoppable. The passion they have for the work they get to do, the impact they are making, and the life that they are creating for themselves is the driving force of their inner fire and brings an energy that feels inextinguishable, especially in the first year of business.

With this influx of energy, it's easier for them to wake up early and work later, because their work is exciting and fulfilling, and they have no problems pushing themselves to their limits in the name of the mission. They can easily juggle their home life, business life, and personal commitments, and they feel like they are on top of the world.

What budding entrepreneurs often don't realize is this influx of energy will not sustain them through the years of their business growth. Without having a plan for boundaries in place, the big mental energy drainers (stress, overwhelm, people-pleasing) that come with entrepreneurship can take over, and we can easily end up in a place of burnout.

Boundaries protect your physical and emotional well-being. Just like you set boundaries with your children, or with people in your life, you must set boundaries that will ensure a good relationship with your business—if you start practicing this now as you enter your first year of business, you will save yourself years of aggravation and self-correction. The setting, balancing, and honoring of boundaries are vitally important to the success of your business growth.

BOUNDARIES: YOUR NEW BUSINESS MODEL

When creating a business model, budding entrepreneurs generally focus on plans for marketing and sales, and on building the infrastructure they need to help them achieve their goals and vision for long-term success. They may have a long-term plan for the revenue goals, their team, and the operations, but may not have thought about what they will need to do to sustain their energetic and physical well-being as they grow. When we are clear on our needs as business owners, we can incorporate boundaries in our business that allow us to stay healthy, serve and lead as our best selves, and grow a healthy, thriving business that we love.

DETERMINE YOUR NON-NEGOTIABLES

When considering our boundaries in business, begin by considering the things that are non-negotiable. Non-negotiables are limits around how we spend our time and use our energy, so we can protect the things in our life that we are not willing to trade, give up, or compromise for our business. Examples are dedicated time with your family every night, health/fitness time, volunteer time at your child's school, time spent reading or learning, or with your pet. Perhaps you play a sport, attend a book club or a bible study, take a class, or love to paint. A non-negotiable could even be committing to four-day work weeks. As business owners, we get to call our own shots.

Your non-negotiables will be the pillars of your business boundaries and one of the first ways you step into the leadership of your business, as you will always be able to protect the things that you value most, even in the midst of compromise.

What are your non-negotiables? Take a few minutes to write down the things that matter most to you and prioritize them. You can always adjust this list as you grow.

TIME BOUNDARY: PROTECT THE WAY YOU SPEND YOUR TIME

Having strong boundaries around your time is a major key to business success. As a business owner, you can create a schedule that accommodates the lifestyle that you want for yourself, so you are working around your life, and not living your life in the leftover pockets of time. When you have time boundaries in place, you are more organized and efficient with your use of time and can prioritize the things that matter most to you.

Once you are clear on your non-negotiables, time-block activities on your calendar now so they are in place and accounted for, and then you can organize your work time around your personal commitments. Sticking to this plan will prevent you from burning out and ensure that you have the energy you need to in order to follow through on your commitments and have time left over to fit in social time, special events, travel, and other things that come up along the way. This also gives you a clear picture of the time you have available to take on new clients or work, and where you can move things around if/when you need to compromise.

ENERGETIC BOUNDARIES AND SELF CARE

Entrepreneurs are often compared to marathon runners. Both create plans that will allow them to sustain the mental effort it takes to run the distance before them. They will not make it through a marathon if they are burned out or running on empty, as burnout leaves us too weak to withstand the challenges that come with entrepreneurship.

Our personal energy is what pushes us to perform in our work to achieve the goals we set ; it is the driving force of our lives and business, and when we run out of it, things can spiral out of control quickly. By having boundaries in place to nurture our energy, we instead have the stamina and resilience to stand strong and maintain the leadership of our business, while we navigate the inevitable challenges that come along the entrepreneurial journey (and life).

When you have dedicated time for the things that fulfill you most, and you are taking care of your body and making time for yourself, you are grounded and have necessary energy for all of your commitments because you are managing yourself wisely. You are clear and high-vibrational, and you attract more opportunities and abundance. You are able to successfully give more energy to projects that need it because you know when to take a break and rest/recharge.

What are some things in your life that give you energy? Think about the things that bring you joy, laughter, gratitude, peace, fulfillment, and creative flow. Write them down.

Boundaries are essential to lead a thriving business. With some practice, you will truly be able to maintain a lifestyle you love while you lead a thriving business. You will stay grounded, have self-trust, have more confidence in your decisions, be able to create and lead from a place of service and not attachment, and have the resilience to withstand the waves of entrepreneurship.

Key Takeaways

- Figure out your non-negotiables, such as self-care, business, and family time.
- Create mindful boundaries that support your energy, life, and goals. Then keep them!
- Write a script in advance for how to address any boundary violations that happen.

Building Unshakeable Trust in Yourself

Lee Murphy Wolf

HAVING A BUSINESS HAS BEEN THE BIGGEST PERSONAL development container I've ever stepped into. It accelerated my personal growth, and I've learned so much about myself, my craft, and my clients.

Over my ten plus years as a coach and strategist for high-achieving, soul-led women, what I discovered is that you don't have to know everything to be good entrepreneur. The one thing you do need to have is unshakeable self-trust.

When you trust yourself, you feel confident in your own abilities, qualities, and judgment. You have clarity and confidence in your choices because they come from your inner authority. When you don't trust yourself, you can become disconnected from your business, and why you started it in the first place.

When you're first starting out, passion is your guide. You're completely inspired and have faith that you will change the world with your work. You believe that you are here to make a difference, and to make great money doing something you love.

As you start to bring your vision to life, self-doubt can set in. There's so much to learn and do. Things don't always go as planned.

Maybe your family thinks you're crazy. Or you find it hard to explain what you do. Or you're not sure what to offer. Or you're not bringing in the money you thought you would make yet.

The conversation in your head may sound something like this, *I really want to serve people, but how do I make money doing that? Who am I to do this? Am I really an expert?*

You may think that your discomfort is a sign that you're not ready. But the truth is, it's part of the process.

When you start a business, you're saying "yes" to yourself. You are answering the call to grow and expand. With that comes taking risks. It takes a lot of courage and commitment. And like anything else that's new, it can feel awkward until you get the hang of it.

When you trust yourself as an entrepreneur, your business reflects that back to you. You own your expertise and price your services in a way that shows you value yourself. You can show up authentically and share your message and your truth. You design your business to align with your values and lifestyle. And you're able to set healthy boundaries and say "no" to people and projects that are a mismatch.

Years ago, I was at an event for coaches and service-based business owners. Twelve coaching industry luminaries were on stage, evaluating contestants' business pitches for expansion.

A contestant was called to the stage. He described his vision and waited for feedback. Several luminaries brainstormed at once, morphing what he shared into a massive empire with multiple income streams, platforms, and audiences.

In the middle of this, one of the luminaries got very quiet. I could feel him feeling into the energy of the exchange. Then he asked the contestant a pivotal question. "Is this what you want?"

The contestant paused. Thoughtfully, he said, "No, it isn't."

The room went silent. You could hear a pin drop. The other luminaries stopped dead in their tracks.

After that, the conversation took a completely different direction. The entrepreneur received amazing advice that was aligned for him and his vision. He began to relax and glow. By the time he left the stage, he appeared exuberant and pulsing with possibility.

It goes to show what can happen for you when you follow your inner compass.

Everyone has an inner compass. It's what keeps you on course in life and in business.

When you trust yourself, you follow your inner compass. You know who you are, and what matters to you. Your core values become your primary filter for making decisions. When your choices are aligned with your core values, you can design your business in a way that feels good to you. Take the time to get clear on where you stand, and what matters most to you. Otherwise, you'll wind up off course and create someone else's version of success.

There's a lot of advice out there about building and protecting your confidence, especially when you're a new entrepreneur. In the beginning, many people get hung up on the idea that they don't have enough experience in their chosen path. This thinking causes so many newer coaches and service providers to underprice their services. But the truth is, you know more than you think you do.

To get where you are now, remember that you've invested many hours in professional training, and more than likely, have worked with dozens of people while you were in school to earn your certification. If you're in a serviced business, you may have interned or done pro bono work to gain experience.

The biggest difference between you and someone who's been doing the same thing that you do in their own business is that they've been at it longer, and you just haven't gotten paid for it yet! As you get out there, you'll close that gap. Everyone starts where they start. It does not make your work less valuable.

If you feel wobbly about this, take stock of your inner wisdom. That's all of the accumulated gold from your life lessons, your intuitive sense of what's needed to help others, your prior professional experience and any training you may have completed. All of it counts. It's what makes you unique and sets you apart as a human being, and from anyone else in your field. That's who you really are, and where the core of your confidence stems from. If you trust in that, you'll be able to firmly ground yourself in your leader energy and create a strong foundation for your success.

We live in a world where we are constantly receiving an inflow of other people's opinions. As a new entrepreneur, you'll be on a learning curve to acquire new skills to help you run your business and will receive lots of advice from different sources. All this mental activity and information can keep you in your head. When you think too much, it can get in the way of trusting yourself.

If you find yourself overthinking, get out of your head and back into your body. Instead of asking yourself what you think, focus on what you feel, and what your body is telling you. There are many simple ways to reconnect to yourself. You can use breathwork, meditate, take a walk, or change your environment.

My personal favorite—the one that I primarily use with my clients—is listening to the simple, yet powerful, frequencies of tuning forks. Doing this helps you to quiet your mind. From that place, you can tap into your intuition with little to no effort. When you can reliably tap in, you develop a better understanding of your intuitive language. When you listen to your inner wisdom, it helps you build trust in your own instincts when making decisions.

Just because I trust myself doesn't mean everything that I decide turns out the way I envisioned it. Nor does it mean that everything I try works. What it does mean is that I have a deep belief that nothing's broken, and all is well. Sometimes it means winding up in Albuquerque when I meant to go to Spokane. That's the beauty of it! That detour will stretch you and can open up opportunities you never would have thought of if the Universe left you to your own devices.

When you have a moment of self-doubt, it's usually because there's something you're afraid of. Rather than focus on what could go wrong, ask yourself, "What can I learn from this?" You can keep your balance by staying fluid. Go with the flow instead of bracing against your own experience. That's the path of least resistance.

It's okay to not know all the answers. And you may not always do the right things. That's part of the process. Instead of trying to get everything right, be a good self-observer and learn from your experiences. Be kind and respectful to yourself, regardless of the outcome of your efforts, and ask for help when you need it.

Above all else, never give up on yourself.

Your business is a living, breathing container. As you evolve, your business will evolve with you. The more you work with clients, the more insights you'll have. Those experiences drive your growth. It's natural for your offers and business model to take a different shape as your business grows. But just because you *can* do something doesn't mean you *should*. If something is not aligned for you, release it with love, and move on.

You know in your heart what you're called to do. You have so much passion, wisdom, creativity, heart and soul to share. Give yourself permission and start where you start. The world needs you and your gifts.

KEY TAKEAWAYS

- The work you do on yourself and for yourself will result in amazing things happening externally.
- You have an internal compass that's always guiding you; trust it!
- Focus on just your next step, not the entire staircase. Give yourself permission to begin today, right where you are.

Part Two
FOUNDATIONS

Five Keys to Launching a Legally Sound Business

Cheri D. Andrews, Esq.

IT'S THE OPPORTUNITY MARY HAD BEEN DREAMING ABOUT—THE thing that had kept her in her underpaid and unappreciated position for years. Mary had worked her tail off in anticipation of a well-deserved promotion. Her entire department thought she was a shoe-in. So, when the company announced that the position went to someone else, it was the proverbial straw that broke the camel's back. Mary quit on the spot.

Mary felt immensely relieved. And excited! She had a great idea for a new business. And the PERFECT name! She was ready to go! Mary spent thousands on a professionally designed logo and website. She printed business cards, purchased domain names, and splurged on company-branded polo shirts and water bottles. She ran Facebook and Google ads, bringing traffic to her website, building her customer list and garnering sales. Over a few years Mary spent tens of thousands, but she built a thriving business. Sales were through the roof. She was more successful than her wildest dreams!

Until one day Mary received a Cease and Desist letter claiming that Mary was infringing the owner's registered trademark. Mary engaged an attorney and found out that, sure enough, this other company owned a registered trademark for her business name.

Not only could Mary no longer use the name and logo she spent so much to design and promote, she was forced to pay the trademark owner all the profits she earned while using that name. Mary had to ditch her website, business name, logo, and branded promotional items, and start from scratch. Ouch!

To make matters worse, Mary operated as a sole proprietor. She had never talked to an attorney or considered establishing a separate business entity. Her company didn't have sufficient funds to pay the settlement award. So, Mary had to empty her own savings account and dip into her retirement funds to pay off the trademark owner.

It's unfortunate, but this precise scenario has bankrupted many a small business! Mary's tale is a cautionary one for all entrepreneurs.

When you move into entrepreneurship, you become the captain of your own ship, the CEO, the BOSS. Your entrepreneurial spirit is a key component to taking that first step in the direction of your dreams. But, before you launch your ship, you need to make sure that the gas tank is full and you have all the provisions you need for a successful journey. That means you need these five keys in place to ensure your small business is legally sound.

Key One

The first key to launching a legally sound business is to **choose your business entity**. In the business world, the business entity is your boat, the container that holds your company. For small business owners, there are two primary reasons to set up a business entity: (1) to protect your personal assets and (2) to minimize your tax liability.

So what entity should you choose? The difference between a sole proprietorship, LLC, or C Corp can affect the trajectory and growth opportunities for your business. The choice should align with your business goals and objectives. Is it going to be just you, or are you planning to scale up and sell your business in the future? Are you self-funding or will you need venture capital? Your intended size and scope matters. Talk to your accountant and your attorney about which entity is right for you.

For many small businesses starting out, the Limited Liability Company (LLC) is the best fit. It offers protection for your personal assets without all the extra work and complications (shareholders, board of directors, corporate minutes, etc.) of a corporation. And the profits pass through to your personal income tax, meaning the tax structure is the same as being a sole proprietor. If Mary had established an LLC, her individual savings and retirement funds would have been safe!

KEY TWO

The second key to launching a legally sound business – **don't go it alone**! Many entrepreneurs make the mistake of thinking they can (or have to) do *everything* themselves. As the captain of your ship, you need a crew to help you on your journey. Your crew will fill the gaps for the skills you don't have, or the tasks you simply don't have the time to handle. For example, it may be more efficient to outsource your bookkeeping or your social media management, and instead spend your time on your income producing activity.

Unless you have the training or specialized knowledge, there are four areas where I strongly encourage you to have a member on your crew advising you: legal, insurance, finances, and taxes. In each of these areas, an innocent mistake could sink your ship and wipe out everything you have worked so hard to build. Or even land you in jail!

Many entrepreneurs make the mistake of thinking their business is too small to need these professionals. Or that legal and financial help can wait until they are making more money. But the truth is that the money you spend up front on professional help can help your business grow and make money faster. And save you many times as much in legal fees and regulatory fines. Having these professionals on your crew helps you mitigate risk and avoid trouble.

KEY THREE

The third key to launching a legally sound business is to *use contracts*. Of course, you *can* run your business on handshake and verbal agreements. People have been doing it for thousands of years. Unfortunately, using a poorly drafted contract, or no contract at all, can leave you exposed to legal risks that are easily avoidable. Using a solid contract, on the other hand, sets clear expectations between the parties and provides the opportunity to include legal protections that you don't get with a verbal or handshake agreement. And those legal protections? Many "templates" available online don't include them at all.

Having a contract in place avoids the problems inherent with ending up in court in a "he said/she said" situation that requires you to prove the terms of your verbal agreement. Without a written agreement, that's a losing proposition! So, get a contract drafted that is customized to your industry and the way you do business. A good business attorney can create a template that allows you to simply change the date, name of the client, and the specific deliverables and cost for each client.

KEY FOUR

The fourth key to launching a legally sound business is to have **plans for compliance** through business Policies and Operating Procedures. You are never too small to need policies for your business!

Most of the policies you will establish for your business are driven by the need to comply with statutes, rules, and regulations. Do/Will you have a website that collects metrics, email addresses, or other personal information? You need to comply with a myriad of consumer privacy laws. Do/Will you have an email marketing list? You need to comply with the CAN-SPAM Act. Employees? There are a host of laws and regulations on that! There are also industry specific regulations to consider.

If this all sounds daunting or scary, just know that your business attorney can answer questions about what regulations are applicable to *your* business; you don't have to figure this out on your own!

KEY FIVE

The fifth key to launching a legally sound business is *respecting Intellectual Property* (IP). When it comes to Intellectual Property, entrepreneurs may unknowingly infringe the IP of others, or fail to protect their own IP. From the trademark on your business name to the copyright registration of your book, course, or blog posts, your intellectual property assets are important parts of your business that deserve protection!

If you didn't have a professional trademark clearance search done before you started using your name, logo, or tagline, you may be unknowingly infringing on someone else's registered mark. You don't want to end up on the receiving end of a Cease & Desist letter. So, get the clearance search done *before* you implement your name, logo, or tagline. Can you imagine how much heartache Mary could have avoided if she had talked to a business attorney before launching her brand? Once you've cleared your brand identity and started using it, take the steps to protect it.

Making sure these five keys are in place positions your business for smooth sailing and a successful journey! Please don't allow the sometimes scary, consistently confusing, and occasionally over-whelming legal aspects of starting and running a small business keep you from sharing your brilliance with the world. You've read this far. You clearly have the desire to run your business in a legally sound way. I applaud you for taking the steps to make that happen! I believe that the world needs your brilliance; it needs your light to shine

brightly and guide the way for others who need what you uniquely
have to share.

Key Takeaways

- Create a firm foundation for your business by choosing a
  registering a business entity.
- Gather a team of professionals to help you navigate areas
  outside your own skill set.
- Use contracts to set clear expectations and provide legal
  protections.
- Ensure compliance with regulations through established
  policies and procedures.
- Protect your intellectual property and make sure you are
  not infringing others!

Get Your Business Books Started Right

Connie Jo Miller

I AM OFTEN SURPRISED BY THE NUMBER OF PEOPLE WHO START A business they are passionate about, without spending much time thinking or doing anything about the money stuff that goes with it. If this is true for you, you aren't alone. Just ask yourself these questions:

1. Do you love numbers and math?
2. Do you like doing detailed, repetitive tasks?
3. Do you love tax time?

If you answered *yes* to all these questions, you might enjoy keeping your books as you start and grow your business. However, if you answered *no* or *not so much*, there are still steps you can take to get started on the right foot.

KEEP YOUR BUSINESS AND PERSONAL MONEY SEPARATE

This means opening a business checking account, a business savings account, and a business credit card and using them exclusively for your business.

If you've already done this, yeah!

You probably started your business using personal money from personal accounts to pay for the first "must haves" for your new business. Things like paying an attorney to help you set up your entity, having a logo designed, having business cards printed, buying a domain name for your website... the list goes on and on. As soon as possible, start using your business accounts for all your business transactions. Don't be tempted to deposit income directly into a personal account. There will be more on that later.

Start a spreadsheet or a list on a piece of paper with a column for the date, the amount spent, exactly what it was for and whether you used business or personal money. Include **everything** you spent money on, even pens, paper, toner or a mouse pad. Don't forget to include personal money you deposit to open your new business accounts. This list will be important at tax time. Even better still, follow the next tip.

OPEN AN ACCOUNTING SOFTWARE ACCOUNT

There are many accounting software options to choose from, but my favorite is QuickBooks Online.

Investpopedia.com frequently reviews all the available software options and can help you decide which one is best for you. Cost, ease of use, features, integrations and the ability to grow as your business does are all considered in their review.

Many new business owners (and even some who have been in business for a while) are reluctant to use accounting software. "A spreadsheet works just fine for me," is an all-too-common comment I hear. Fear of learning yet another software, not wanting to spend the money and hidden money blocks are a few of the reasons for this.

But the beauty of using accounting software is the ability you gain to connect your business accounts to the software, which means all your transactions will be automatically uploaded. If you are diligent about using only your business accounts for business purchases, all your expenses will be captured in one place. You won't miss any business expenses, which means you won't miss legitimate deductions on your taxes. As transactions come into your account, you learn to categorize them by deciding which "bucket" they belong in. Is it income or an expense? If it's an expense, what kind of expense? You can make your expense categories roughly line up with the lines of the Schedule C used for reporting the Profit and Loss for your business at tax time.

STAY CONSISTENT WITH HOW YOU CATEGORIZE TRANSACTIONS

Always put similar transactions into the same category.

Let's say you have a transaction on your credit card for your website hosting. That should go to a "website expense" subcategory under "marketing expense." If you can't remember how you categorized it before, do a search in your accounting software to see how you have categorized it previously and stay consistent.

KEEP A LIST

Keep a list of all your subscriptions, memberships, and ongoing expenses. We are inundated with apps, programs, software and "this is the way you do it" courses when we first start a business. It's easy to spend, spend, spend when you have so many options, each better than what you already have of course. It's also easy to forget *what* you already have and then find out it auto-renewed last week. Yikes!

Keep this list up to date, look at it at least quarterly, and remember to include the length of the commitment and renewal dates. Put reminders on your calendar for a couple of weeks before renewal dates so that you can make a decision about renewing or not.

Are you aware of all the features in the apps and software you are using? Look for overlaps in features and purpose. Do you really need two CRMs?

Be watchful for "one more class-itis." Imposter syndrome is real and leads to over-committing to classes and courses – another recurring expense. Trust that you know enough, trust that when you really need help you will know. Stop falling for "this is the only way that works" courses.

Do invest in apps that help you run your business efficiently. Do invest in courses that give you knowledge you lack. Do keep track of these expenses that can sneak up on you and eat up all your profit.

KEEP RECORDS OF YOUR EXPENSES

Decide how you are going to keep track of your documentation and be consistent. No, a shoe box doesn't count. Digital is best.

Keep all documentation that shows how you have spent money. This includes:

- Invoices
- Bills
- Receipts
- Bank and credit card statements, including canceled checks
- Tax returns
- 1099s

UPDATE YOUR BOOKS REGULARLY

Work on your books either weekly, biweekly, or monthly. Pick what works for you and stick with it. Pick a day of the week and a time when you don't have any ongoing commitments, then block it on your calendar. Pick whatever you feel you can be consistent with.

Biweekly is a good place to start. A lot can happen in a month, so that's too long to go without looking at your books. Weekly is great but shoot for *at least* biweekly. Put updating your books as a recurring task on your calendar.

. . .

CREATE A PROCESS

A process can be a few simple steps that you use to do your books.

Log into your accounting software, update your transactions to bring everything up to date. Start categorizing your transactions. I usually do expenses first and save the fun part for last: Income! Do whatever works for you.

If you get stuck, there are many tutorials on YouTube. You can also work with a bookkeeper to help you with software basics and improve your confidence.

Write down each step of your process as you go. Or better yet – record yourself as you work through a session of doing your books. There's nothing worse than figuring out how to do something and then the next time it comes up, you can't remember how you did it.

PAY YOURSELF

When you first start your business, it's easy to put any money you make back into the business. That's okay for a while, but the IRS expects you to be in business to make money. There are several factors the IRS considers when determining if you are a business or a hobby. For example, one threshold is "the taxpayer depends on income from the activity for their livelihood." Check out this link to see the other factors the IRS uses: https://www.irs.gov/newsroom/heres-how-to-tell-the-difference-between-a-hobby-and-a-business-for-tax-purposes.

SAVE MONEY FOR TAXES

Regularly put aside money in your business savings account for paying your quarterly taxes. The first year, you typically won't pay a penalty if you don't make quarterly tax payments. But, if you are making gobs of money, pay quarterly taxes so you won't have a big bill due at tax time.

GET HELP WITH YOUR BOOKS

When you can afford it, or even when you don't think you can quite afford it, hire someone to keep your books. This gives you more time to work in your zone of brilliance. It also relieves stress, guilt and overwhelm. Hiring the right bookkeeper sends a message to the Universe: I am ready for more clients. I am ready for the next step!

WHAT YOU PAY ATTENTION TO GROWS

I have many stories from solopreneurs I have worked with that almost right away started increasing their bottom line. Expenses go down and more income starts rolling. A multiple six-figure client recently realized that she had made as much in the first six months of this year as she had made all of last year.

Pay attention to your numbers, learn what your financial statements mean and learn what they tell you about the health of your business. Please don't do your books annually on the day before taxes are due! The stress, overwhelm, and shame of being behind just isn't worth it. Pay attention and magic will happen.

KEY TAKEAWAYS

- Keep your business and personal finances separate. Always. In all ways.
- Put a recurring appointment on your calendar to regularly review your financial statements.
- Celebrate your financial wins—even the smallest wins are worth celebrating!

Having a Heart of Service

Laura Templeton

HE STOOD AMID A SEA OF PEOPLE PATIENTLY SHUFFLING ALONG waiting to experience Space Mountain. To my brothers and I, it felt like the line was taking forever. But not to Dad. Nope, there he was chatting away with the people in front of him and behind him, and each time the line would move, he'd include the people on either side too. Pretty soon they were laughing, telling jokes and acting like old friends. He just kept gathering people into the conversation as we'd do the cattle chute shuffle.

My young mind, in a state of frenzied wonder, tried to figure out how my dad had so many friends, and how they all knew to show up at Disney World and get in line for Space Mountain at the same time as my family. I was amazed that all my dad's friends could take off from work and bring their families on vacation at the same time. It was only later, when I asked Dad if his friends were coming to dinner, that I found out he had just met those people. I'll never forget the twinkle in his eyes when he said, "Lines move faster for everyone when you make it fun."

Who knew that lesson I learned from my dad while lining up for

Space Mountain would be so helpful during my first year of entrepreneurship?

When I started my journey as an entrepreneur, I focused on meeting as many people as possible to share what *I* had to offer, because I knew if I did, they would all buy from me.

Or so I thought.

I chose networking as my key marketing strategy. I thought I would attend meetings, meet people and sell my stuff. Imagine my surprise when I realized networking wasn't at all what I had expected. In fact, it was so much more than I had ever imagined. Networking taught me how to be a better business owner and a better human.

Like my dad, I love meeting new people and hearing their stories. I love getting to know them. I love figuring out how I can support them and who I can connect them with.

Connecting people is one of the easiest ways to serve the people in your network. News flash: not everyone is going to be your client, but you may come across someone who is a perfect fit for *someone else* in your networking community.

Thinking back to that line at Space Mountain, and countless other encounters, my dad taught me how to be a great listener and communicator. Dad was amazing at connecting with people, and it wasn't just because of his great smile or his infectious laughter. It was because he genuinely cared about and was interested in others. As a result, Dad knew how to ask great questions that engaged people in conversation with ease.

Essentially, Dad was a collector of people. He had a way of making people feel welcome, heard, and remembered. By watching my dad, I learned at a very young age how to engage with people and how to have great conversations. Now, one thing you need to know about me is that I am an ambivert. I can be very withdrawn until I get to know people. Much of the time I'll join a new networking group, and I'm the quietest person in the room. But after a few months, after

I've opened up and built relationships, people usually comment about how engaging I've become.

Even though I'm an ambivert, I still made a lot of connections and had great conversations, which were critical during my first year in business. These skills—the ability to communicate well and connect with people—helped me find key people to support me on my journey and the clients that needed my help. In my business practice as a brand communications consultant and speaker, I teach audiences to embrace the art of being a great connector.

And what I believe makes someone a great connector is this: the desire to put others' needs and feelings before your own.

That's one of the things that I loved about watching my dad; he just wanted to make people feel good. By his example, I learned that I could help people to feel good by having great conversations and learning about what they do, what they like and what lights them up about life. I love connecting them with other people or making introductions when someone new enters the room or on social media. You learn to see how somebody might be a good connection for someone else because they serve similar clients and do similar work, and you see collaborative opportunities in the making.

Not everyone will be your client, so how else can you help them? By becoming a great connector, a collector of people. This is an amazing way to help the people in your community, and this comes from having a heart of service. Having a heart of service simply means having a desire and a willingness to help others succeed.

The one thing I discovered when I stopped focusing on selling, and started focusing on helping others, is that they did the same for me. They started connecting me with networking groups, potential clients, conference planners and other consultants with the same clients as mine. One gentleman who wanted to support me purchased two cases of my book, 30 *Second Success: Ditch the pitch and start connecting!*, for his local LeTip chapter. Not only did he see the value of my work, he saw how it would benefit the people that he cared about. It's amazing to experience that level of connection with the people in your network.

I would encourage you to become a great communicator, a great connector, and a collector of people! Serve others with all your heart, take the onus off selling and start serving others in a way that's compassionate, compelling and communicative. When you have a heart of service, you're in tune with what the people around you need.

Find out what pain or problem they may be struggling with and then determine if you or someone you know has a solution. Then help them get what they need. Become intentional about understanding what the people in your network do. Take the time to get to know the people that you're connecting with, whether it's in person, virtual or on social media. Don't think of them as prospects. One of the most fatal mistakes we make when first launching a business is thinking that everyone's a potential client.

Remember, not everyone needs your services, but many need you to help them grow, and in turn, they want to do the same for you. They have a desire to help the people in their networking community get what they need, too. There's a quote that says, "A rising tide lifts all boats," which refers to setting an example for others to follow. It's how we grow... together. When we work together as a community, it is important to know what everyone does and how they serve their clients. This knowledge comes from having frequent conversations, showing interest and gaining a deep understanding of what the people in your network do. This type of connection is a beautiful testimony to the people you choose to surround yourself with.

A question I'm often asked is how I keep all my connections organized after more than seven years in business, and to be honest with you, it isn't easy. Taking good notes when meeting with people helps with recall. I also add people to my contacts and include the type of service they offer in the notes section for searchability.

Making introductions in the moment has become an essential practice these days as I connect with more people. By keeping

LinkedIn open during a call or meeting, I can quickly send a message to a contact telling them that they should connect with the person I am on the call with. Here's an example of a quick introduction:

> *Clare meet Hanne, Hanne meet Clare. I believe the two of you should connect. Clare just mentioned needing help with visual branding and knowing your work Hanne, I wouldn't send her to anyone else. Happy connecting!*

Communicating and connecting doesn't have to be hard or complicated, it just has to be memorable.

Key Takeaways

- Growing your people network enriches your life and your business.
- When you listen for what others want and need you can help them get it.
- As a collector of people, be purposeful about making introductions.
- Serve from the heart. Shift your focus from selling to serving with heartfelt connections.

Looking the Part from the Start
Hanne Brøter

IT IS SAID THAT WE SHOULD NOT "JUDGE THE BOOK BY THE cover," but we do. Consciously or not, we base our perception, and even judgment of things, on their visual appearance. Even as a start-up, you'll want your business to be perceived as remarkable.

Starting out on a budget, you may have no choice but to refrain from hiring a graphic designer for a full-fledged visual branding process. Fair enough. The alternative is to execute what I call "informed DIY," which means teaching yourself some simple but invariable facts about graphic design and visual branding and acting according to them.

You can become competent in graphic design and visual branding decisions. Instead of plunging headlong into the Canva "buffet," seek to understand basic principles of graphic design and visual branding. Establish a knowledge base as your starting point, from which you can advance step-by-step on the right paths toward your future fully-developed visual brand. This will prevent you from having to pivot entirely, trashing all your previously self-concocted stash and starting over from scratch. You will also be able to communicate clearly when you are ready to enter into a co-creational relationship with a professional graphic designer. This will save time, frustration, and money.

Your visual brand is the visible professional reputation of your business. It precedes you and signals on your behalf what kind of business you run. A prominent professional reputation cannot be achieved with shabby visual branding and bad graphic design.

What is Visual Branding?

The first thing people think about as visual branding is visual consistency. And consistency is undoubtedly *one* essential part of it, but there are also two equally important parts, about which most people are unaware. Below are the three fundamental parts of visual branding:

1. Original authenticity
2. Visual consistency
3. Correct graphic design

These are interdependent, so having just one of the three will be inadequate. You want to leverage all three to make your brand stand out as trustworthy, serious, and professional.

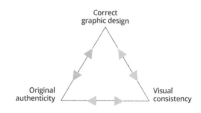

It is Not About You, It is About Them

A common beginner mistake is to regard yourself as the receiver of your own visual communication. People tend to choose the visual means they love the most, which is okay in your home decoration of which you are the prime end-user. Your visual branding, however, is not about you. It is about your potential client or customer, the person you want to attract via your website, your brochures, your advertisements, your business card or your social media graphics. Do you know if she has exactly the same taste as *you?* Obviously, you must be able to identify with your visual means. You cannot issue into the world visuals and graphics you hate. But always have your clients in mind.

ORIGINAL AUTHENTICITY

To brand anything, we must know exactly what "it" is. It is necessary to figure out "who" your business is. As an entrepreneur, you need to have an identity-conversation with yourself.

The visual part of your branding is the visual representation of the brand itself. We cannot give any brand a visual appearance without first describing it in words. Entrepreneurs often have problems clearly describing who they are, what they do, for whom they do it and what they want to achieve. If they can't explain these things in straightforward language to themselves, they have no hope of explaining it to others.

You must find the words to describe:

- Why you do what you do;
- What your mission is;
- What your values and visions are;
- How you would like to be perceived; and
- Who your ideal customer is.

At this point we are not working with visual things like colors or fonts, but with thoughts, ideas and words. Later you will translate these words into a visual language.

. . .

VISUAL CONSISTENCY

Deciding on a set of colors, fonts and imagery, and using it consistently across all your marketing materials will make your business recognizable everywhere. It is your visual voice, by which people will know, like and trust you.

Don't tumble into the pitfall of "patchwork branding." Don't be tempted by features in your software to try out different colors, fonts, images, templates and "design-ideas" in each piece you are creating. Make it easy for people to remember you when they need your kind of service. If you turn up in different arenas in different costumes every time, people will not remember you.

Translating your original authenticity into visual means that represent the unique personality of your business is one of the special skills of a trained graphic designer. If you aren't ready yet to hire a graphic designer, I have some suggestions for you below.

Getting a visual profile in place will bring your business a giant step closer to appearing professional, trustworthy and serious. However, neither original authenticity nor visual consistency can carry the weight of your visual branding by themselves, we need the third ingredient, which we'll look at next.

CORRECT GRAPHIC DESIGN

Failing to use correct graphic design is the most common mistake in DIY visual branding.

Graphic design and typography are specialist areas with their own rules and guidelines whose purposes are to make the message come across in the clearest way possible.

Correct graphic design is using the means of graphic design in accordance with the principles of graphic design.

- The means of graphic design are colors, letters, images
  and layout
- The five principles of graphic design are contrast, space,
  alignment, repetition, and direction.

If you aren't aware of these principles and create your content
without using them, you deprive your message of the probability of
coming across clearly. Your piece will feel out of balance and unpro-
fessional. Only a few people will be able to describe exactly what
causes this feeling of unbalanced improperness. Aim to inform yourself to become one of those who can.

This is not a skill that can be gained by using templates or techni-
cally mastering a graphic design software like Canva, InDesign, or
PowerPoint. This is about *knowing and understanding* the basic rules
of graphic design and training your eyes to *see* when you are violating
them and adjusting accordingly. The most important tools in graphic
design are your eyes and your brain.

A Few Words About Logos

Your logo is the most important part of your Visual Branding.
Logo design is the one area where I strongly recommend you seek
assistance from a graphic designer. Here are three essential require-
ments to consider:

1. **Will the logo look good even in small sizes on
   a screen?** Today the primary use of logos is digital. The
   size allowed for rendering a logo online is usually tiny.
   The clearer, less complicated or entangled the logo is, the
   greater its chances of withstanding digital downscaling.
2. **Will the logo lose impact or information when
   rendered in only one color?** Sometimes, it is
   necessary or even preferable that your logo is rendered in
   only one color. The most common example is a white,

transparent logo that you can use on colored backgrounds and images.

3. **Can the logo be "split" into parts that can do the job alone?** I am a huge fan of "logo-ensembles." Think about *Nike* and its name, swoosh and tagline (Just Do It) which are being used individually or in different combinations and sizes across their products and marketing.

Logos should be created as vector files. Every other file format can be generated from these files. Your final logo needs to be issued as JPG and PNG files for all your logo versions (full color, black and white).

Carry out some design management by keeping profile elements like logos, images and graphics in a brand archive on your computer. This step will save you time and money.

If you want to dive deeper into Visual Branding, I recommend my book *Brand Boxes™: Your 9-Step Process to Create a Visually Compelling Brand.* I wish you tremendous success in your business and visual branding endeavors. I believe in you! If you need my support, please reach out to me. Best of luck!

KEY TAKEAWAYS

- Have an identity conversation. Ask a peer to help you identify the right words and be your sounding board. If you have the budget, work with a brand messaging coach.
- Choose between two and five brand colors that you think suit your business. Choose one of them to be your main brand color. Ask for feedback from peers and clients. Choose one-to-two simple, clear and legible fonts and use them consistently.

Part Three
MARKETING

Not Everyone Is Your Client
Jill Celeste, MA

WHEN I STARTED MY FIRST BUSINESS, HOUND DOG SOCIAL Media, I declared myself "open for business," and was ready for clients. I needed income, especially after leaving my corporate job, so I sold my social media services to anyone. Real estate investors, song lyrics companies, RV rental businesses—you name it. If they needed someone to post on Facebook and Twitter for them, I was their girl.

As I helped my clients, though, things weren't clicking. The work burned me out, and I felt scattered. In addition, these clients who claimed they needed my social media services didn't want to pay my rates, so I accepted less that I was worth. Plus, because I served so many different types of businesses, my marketing copy was not hitting the mark. After six months of low pay and less-than-enthusiastic client relationships, I worried if I was cut out for entrepreneurship. I didn't want to go back to corporate, though, so I needed to figure it out.

That's when I took a deep breath and thought about my predicament like a Director of Marketing for a large company would. I have years of corporate marketing experience, so I put on my "marketing hat" and pretended I was working with a client. What would I say to this client if she was in the same situation?

The answer came to me like a lightning bolt. My biggest and most urgent problem was this: *I believed everyone was my ideal client.*

It was like a proverbial slap to the forehead. Of course! That made so much sense! Why was I working with *everyone*? Shouldn't I be selective and have criteria for who I work with?

Admittedly, I had some initial doubts about narrowing down who I would help because I feared I would miss income opportunities. However, I knew from years of corporate marketing experience that I must trust the process because I knew it worked.

Energized, I grabbed my journal and brainstormed who I would *love* to help with their social media marketing. The answers flowed from my pen. I had years of healthcare marketing experience, and I loved working with non-profit healthcare companies. Based on my experience in healthcare marketing and social media, I knew I could help these companies plan and execute an effective social media strategy. As I scribbled my thoughts, I exclaimed to myself, *Now, this is exciting!*

With a firm idea as to who my ideal clients were (and who they were not), I rewrote my website copy, changed my visual branding, and emailed all of my healthcare contacts. One by one, healthcare companies hired me. Not only were they ideal clients, they also *valued* by work, which meant I got paid more for my talents. Win, win, win!

Even though I do not run Hound Dog Social Media anymore, I will never forget this valuable first entrepreneurial lesson. With every business reiteration I've undertaken—and even with the books I've written—I have always taken the time to get to know who my ideal clients are.

Revered marketer Seth Godin once said, "Everyone is not your customer." Remember this quote because it's true. So, how do you determine who your ideal clients are? Here are four tips to help you.

LOOK AT YOUR OWN JOURNEY

Oftentimes, you are your own ideal client. In fact, you may have started your business because you transformed in some way, and now you want to teach others how to have this same transformation. For example, if you're a health coach who lost weight and lowered your cholesterol, your ideal client may be the same as you—someone who desires to weigh less and have healthier blood test results.

Your ideal client goes through three stages: (1) The "before" state, (2) the "transformation" state, and (3) the "after" stage. Knowing these three steps, think about your journey. What was your life like *before* you began your transformation? What did you do, specifically, to *transform*? Finally, what's your life like now *after* achieving this transformation? Answering these three questions will give you amazing insight into who your ideal clients are (and how you can help them).

ASK YOUR IDEAL CLIENTS

Sometimes, you know someone who is your ideal client, even if you haven't worked with her yet. It may be someone you met through networking or someone in your peer group.

If you know a person who is your ideal client, ask her to fill in the blanks for you. You can do this through a simple email. Tell the recipient you are trying to find more ideal clients—just like her—and ask if she could answer a few questions for you. You can type the questions right in your email or link to a survey (SurveyMonkey, JotForm, or Google Forms are excellent tools for surveys). Most people are happy to help, especially if you keep it short and sweet.

Here are some questions you can ask:

- What is the biggest thing that keeps you up at night?
- What one struggle do you wish you could overcome—knowing if you do, your business/life would be so much better?

- What stops you from overcoming this struggle?
- If money and time were not an issue, and you could invest in someone to help you solve this problem, what result would you look for? In other words, what breakthrough would make you happy?
- If I could go somewhere to meet more people like you, where would I go? What networking groups, associations, and other meetings should I look into?

DEMOGRAPHICS AND PSYCHOGRAPHICS

Now that you have a general idea of who your ideal client is, you need to drill down even more. It's time to delve into the demographics and psychographics of your ideal clients.

In case these are new terms to you, here are their definitions:

- Demographics are the features of a specific population, such as age and location.
- Psychographics are the behavioral and lifestyle features of a specific population, such as interests and opinions.

If you're a visual learner, check out this table to help understand the differences between demographics and psychographics:

Demographics

- Gender
- Interests
- Age
- Attitudes
- Income

Psychographics

- Opinions
- Location
- Biggest struggle or problem
- Marital Status
- Hobbies
- Profession
- Lifestyle

Look back at the research you've already gathered about your ideal client. Analyze this information and organize the data into demographics and psychographics. Don't hesitate to ask your ideal clients to fill in any holes.

As you meet more people—and learn more about your ideal client—your knowledge about her demographics and psychographics will grow. Keep a running list to help you keep track of what you've learned.

Creating Your Ideal Client Persona

Once you determine the psychographics and demographics of your ideal client, create an Ideal Client Persona. In other words, create a profile or client avatar that is the perfect representation of your client.

Here is the flow you can follow when writing your Ideal Client Persona:

1. Start by naming your ideal client. As hokey as it sounds, naming your persona helps others identify with it (because it seems like a real person who is just like her).
2. Consider buying a stock image to add to your persona— some type of photographic representation of your ideal

client (make sure the photo matches the demographics of
your ideal client).

3. Describe who your ideal client is and what her biggest
   problems are.

4. Specify what your ideal client needs to do to solve her
   problems.

Remember: The idea behind writing an Ideal Client Persona is to
get your prospective client to say, "This is me!"

It may take you several revisions to finalize your Ideal Client
Persona—but do not give up. In fact, as long as you're in business, you
will be tweaking—and maybe revamping—your Ideal Client Persona.
That's normal!

Take time to interview your ideal clients to learn the exact
language they are using to describe themselves. This will help you
write an Ideal Client Persona that will make people want to work
with you.

Now that you have a game plan on learning more about your
ideal client, it's time to get to work! Start researching, asking questions, and documenting your findings. Write your ideal client persona
and put it everywhere your ideal client can find it, especially on your
website. When you know who you want to serve and create a persona
that inspires your client to work with you, your business will transform into the prosperous, soul-filling business you've always dreamt
about.

Key Takeaways

- Not everyone is your ideal client. This is an important
  and necessary mindset shift—one that many new
  entrepreneurs struggle with (you are not alone if you're
  feeling this way!).

- Think about *your* journey because often you are your own ideal client. Remember how you felt before your transformation, during the transformation, and afterwards. This is valuable information for understanding your ideal clients.
- Do you know someone who is your ideal client? Consider interviewing her to learn more about her goals and struggles.
- As you gather information about your ideal client, also consider their demographics and psychographics. These characteristics will help you understand your ideal client even more.
- Finally, pull your research and write an ideal client persona, which is a narrative that outlines who your ideal client is and what their big problems are.

Networking: An Unnecessary Evil or An Essential Marketing Tool?

Clare Whalley

OVERAWED. HEART PALPITATIONS. SWEATY PALMS...THESE WERE some of the feelings I experienced attending my first networking event back in 2007, shortly after setting up my business. On reflection, I was a rabbit in the headlights stepping into that space. It was an area set up to emulate a board room experience – just the kind of corporate atmosphere I had desperately escaped from months before – with a long, highly-polished table, lots of older men in gray suits, a cold and serious atmosphere, exceptionally bright lights, and too many seemingly impenetrable small congregations of people chatting quietly.

At least that's how I remember it.

Fast forward fifteen years and I absolutely love networking! And it's now the most successful method of marketing (at a staggering 80% share) my business coaching practice has.

So How Did the Big Shift Happen?

Before delving into my big shift, let's look at a few statistics. According to HubSpot, 86% of jobs are filled through networking

(70% are not even publicly published), followed by parties and social events closing 51% of roles and conferences at 49%.

The impact of COVID has seen 70% of small business owners now doing their networking online. This, of course, may change as time moves on, however, we have definitely experienced a major shift in how we *choose* to network.

And love it or hate it, since its inception in 1985, Business Networking International (BNI), the largest and most successful networking organization in the world, boasts $19.4 billion member-generated revenue.

Bottom line: networking, whether it's face-to-face, online or over a few drinks, is not to be overlooked!

If you fit snugly into my old camp of feeling daunted and overwhelmed at the prospect of *any* kind of networking, or maybe you are networking, but you still feel uncomfortable and you aren't seeing any financial return from your efforts, then listen in to how I transformed my networking practices into something that reaps over 80% of my yearly turnover, so you can replicate the results for your own business.

Realizing I wanted to make my networking efforts reap a financial return for my business, and with a deep desire to get comfortable in networking meetings, I went on a one-woman mission to *gain confidence*.

I had already learned through my NLP (Neuro-linguistic Practitioner) training, that confidence was a learned skill, and having already practiced a handful of NLP strategies, I knew it made a huge difference, although still not big enough for my objectives.

Still with a long way to go, practice and even more practice was the only way to increase my confidence, my self-belief, and my ability to get through that elevator pitch without swallowing at least a hundred times.

Secure in my ability to conquer my fears, I felt that through networking my credibility would grow, and that this would be the key to unlocking the holy grail of clients.

It's important to share at this point, I had very little money coming in and a pretty big mortgage. As it is with most start-ups, time was of the essence.

I visited as many networking groups as money constraints would allow, and substituting for fellow business owners meant that many meetings were free to attend, and often had the added bonus (ahem!) of performing not one, but two, 60-second elevator pitches.

Attending all those meetings revealed the huge range of networking opportunities that were out there, as well as introducing me to groups that had various different approaches, for example:

- *Formal* – standing up to share your elevator pitch
- *Informal* – sitting down to share your business or not even doing a pitch
- *Learning-style meetings* – a speaker sharing their motivational story for start-up success
- *A sharing and caring approach* – where members and guests would share current business challenges and receive the benefit of everyone's expertise around the room.

Boom! All of a sudden, I was able to see networking in a whole new light. To unlock business connections meant learning from those who had been there, seen it and done it, and who were sharing their challenges and successes with like-minded people standing in the metaphorical ring with me.

Once the pressure of "getting business" was taken off the top of the agenda, it became a biproduct of continuous learning, meeting similar people and sharing ideas for better business practices. More clients became the cherry on top.

Plus, I had been so busy learning and feeling new levels of motivation toward marketing my business, I'd missed my confidence levels hitting whole new heights as a by-product.

After spending a year or more attending and chairing different groups, I decided the best way forward was to create my own group. A network that would encompass all the lovely ways of sharing, learning and engaging with like-minded people that I'd seen working brilliantly in other groups and that I already knew would be a perfect fit for me.

"Angels in Business" was born or "Meta4 Business Mastermind" as it has now been rebranded. A network that had everything that *I* needed first and foremost:

- Business owners – check
- Learning – check
- Business goal setting – check
- Interesting, ambitious, open-minded people focused on business growth – check.

My close and regular network is now exclusively filled with business professionals who will listen to other people's challenges and share their own, who will offer practical solutions, and who are eager to learn new growth strategies, while being fun to be with, too!

So, spend some time working out exactly what *you* need from a networking group. Put *you* first and the business will follow.

SOCIAL MEDIA NETWORKING

Social media networking of course has a time and a place but should not be exclusively relied upon to drive all your marketing activity. After all, whichever tech giant owns the platform also owns the email address, the connection and therefore the relationship.

Meeting with people, whether it's in person or online via Zoom, is ultimately where the relationship and trust is built.

Reaching out to my network on LinkedIn, I shared about contributing to this book and asked others to share their networking experiences. The question was of course: *Networking – An Unneces-*

sary Evil or An Essential Marketing Tool? And I had some great responses.

(Side note, all comments were from connections I'd met at face-to-face networking.)

> *"Someone told me to try networking, I knew nothing about it but rocked up with my printed sheet of 60 seconds of waffle! I was utterly terrified, and my hands were shaking when it was my turn! I still got 2 new clients from that first event (even though I'm sure I was terrible). I think personally it is the MOST powerful marketing tool beyond all else, building relationships face to face with real people. And the more you do it, the more you enjoy it."*
>
> — Kate Curry, The Curry Design Studio

NOW KATE WAS LUCKY. I BET THERE AREN'T MANY PEOPLE WHO get business on their first-time networking. But never say never! In any case, eight years into her business and now it's her most powerful marketing tool.

And Karen Kirby, HR, shared her parallels to my experience:

> *"Essential marketing tool. I too have been on that networking journey. But it the sole reason I earn any money."*
>
> — Karen Kirby, HR

IF YOU'RE MARKETING ONLINE, GET THOSE ONLINE conversations offline wherever possible. Meet up for coffee, chat over Zoom, offer free and helpful resources, and add value – anything that takes the connection off the social platform and onto your email list and more closely into your inner networking circle.

. . .

TIME VERSUS RETURN

As a business coach, I hear all the time from fellow business owners who have been part of a network for many years but experience little financial return. So, let's not beat around the bush, and instead refer to this more aptly as "volunteer work," and obviously volunteer work doesn't pay the bills.

It's time to get real. Your network, as well as bringing you joy, camaraderie, motivation, inspiration, learning and so on, should also bring you **business**.

If you don't track your enquiries and marketing efforts, the time to start now. Create yourself a simple spreadsheet. It should look something like this:

1. Marketing Avenue: Networking
2. Time Spent (monthly): 8 hours
3. Financial Return: Income
4. Financial Return minus Time & Resources Spent: Gross profit

Now there's not always a direct correlation between your marketing effort and results, however tracking will start to give you a clearer indication of where your time, resources and investment is best spent.

And if something is not working, *stop doing it* or work out what you need to do differently to start getting the results you are looking for. Speak to your trusted connections and ask for constructive feedback.

In summary, networking for small businesses *is* an essential marketing tool. It's a way in which business owners can make their worlds less insular and more connected, less uninspired, and more innovative, and less feast and famine and more financially stable.

Networking creates a more rounded and fulfilled entrepreneur with a business that will stand the test of time. Isn't that what we all want?

. . .

KEY TAKEAWAYS

- Being part of a vibrant and active networking group will help make your business journey a much less lonely place
- Find the right balance between networking and "not working." Networking can drain your time if you allow it to. Make sure it's reaping a financial return
- Take your networking conversations with like-minded connections to the next level. Meet up for coffee so you can both delve deeper into what the other does. This is where the real business happens.

How to Become a Thought Leader in Your First Year of Business

Pam Knox

IT WAS MY FIRST YEAR OF BUSINESS, AND DESPITE MY DECADE OF experience as a marketing communication leader, I didn't think of myself as a thought leader. I don't even know if that was a thing twenty-six years ago. Yet, just six months into entrepreneurship, I gained recognition as a thought leader. How did I know?

When one industry association leader asked an executive director at another organization if he knew a great marketing communication consultant, the response was "yes, you need to call Pam Knox." In that moment, I had been elevated to "top of mind awareness," which translates as recognition as a thought leader.

My identity as a thought leader gave me confidence as I met with prospective clients during that first year. It is what I leveraged when I met with a prospect to discuss his needs for a newsletter. In his office that day, he began the conversation by putting a copy of his newsletter on the desk in front of me. His "newsletter" was a thirty-two-page magazine complete with paid advertising. My kneejerk response could have been, "I have never published a magazine before." Instead, my mindset fueled me with an internal response that said, *I have not had the opportunity to publish a magazine yet,*

and as a thought leader in marketing communications I can do this. I
secured that client and serviced them for ten years.

THOUGHT LEADERSHIP DEFINED

Stepping into the arena as a thought leader early on in your
entrepreneurial journey will provide a powerful foundation to fuel
your visibility, influence, confidence and expertise.

Demonstrating thought leadership shines a spotlight on you and
your business. It draws people into your circle of influence and
enables you to have more impact.

I have defined thought leadership as *credibility that increases visibility and leads to opportunity.* Though thought leadership is considered by many to be about expertise alone, it is really about the
attachment of voice to that expertise.

Putting forth your voice, sharing a new perspective, contributing
to a discussion or engaging in online commentary is thought leadership in action.

But how does someone become crowned as a "thought leader?"
Becoming a thought leader doesn't require a specific certification or
series of steps like earning a Girl Scouts badge.

Consider for a moment someone who has spoken at a global
conference before an international audience from over 100 countries,
represented leading firms as a spokesperson, was elected president of
an industry trade association and exercised their leadership skills
serving on the board of directors of three non-profits. These statements would make for an impressive resume, however they don't
elevate that individual to the instant status of thought leader.

Positions and job titles do not make you a thought leader. Like-
wise, a college degree or lack thereof doesn't impact whether or not
you get to be a thought leader.

In my work as a strategic communication consultant and coach, I
help entrepreneurs package their thought leadership, create their
messaging strategy and promote their personal brands through

powerful communication. During a one-on-one session with a heart-centered entrepreneur, I asked her questions to gather information to create a bio for her. Listening intently, I gently pulled out insight that was core to her personal brand and added vibrancy to the piece. During this part of the conversation, she was at ease. However, when we got to the part about her degrees and certifications, her body language shifted. Her vibrancy escaped as she became devoid of oxygen from holding her breath. Shrinking like a violet, she disclosed that she didn't have a college degree. I reminded her that thought leadership can exist independent of degrees, certifications, awards or other accolades. Our subsequent coaching sessions enabled her to harness the mindset of a thought leader and confidently uphold those thought leader qualities that resided deep within her very essence. She went on to add writer and public speaker to her now growing list of accolades.

THOUGHT LEADER MINDSET

Leveraging your thought leadership to increase your visibility requires a thought leader mindset. The mindset required of a thought leader reverberates with the voice that says:

- I matter
- I have something of value to share with this community
- Sharing this information ignites me and lights up those around me
- It is my responsibility to share my perspective and expertise in service to others
- My insight is unique and has the power to transform those around me.

THOUGHT LEADERSHIP IS NOT BRANDING

Some folks confuse thought leadership with business branding. Thought leadership is not marketing, but it does take your branding further. As an extension of your brand, your thought leadership should be in alignment and amplify the core messaging of your brand.

For example, if you want your brand to be about authenticity, convey that with your thought leadership. If your business brand is about innovation, anchor your thought leadership and distribute it inside the innovation space or startup ecosystem. Is it your humorous approach that sets you apart? Then, inject some playfulness and fun in your tone or voice as you put yourself out there.

SUBJECT MATTER EXPERTISE

There are a few ways you can find clues as to what subject matter or topics are closely aligned with your areas of expertise. I often recommend to my entrepreneur clients to listen closely to the feedback given by others who point out areas that you excel in. Take notice when you express something, and people lean in to engage.

Another option is to take a pulse and give yourself a heart-centered assessment. What aspects of your work are you passionate about and want the world to know about it? What are the topics or subject areas where you have become the "go-to person?" Do you have a unique perspective or different opinion on these matters?

Here are a few more questions to ask yourself:

- What subjects resonate with you deep inside and prompt the most feedback from clients?
- What topics could you go on and on about because you are so enthusiastic about them?
- What topics could you spend all your free time researching?

- What areas of expertise are so inherent in you that time passes quickly when you are speaking or writing about them?

Thought Leadership is Meant to be Shared

After you determine what subject matters closely align with your unique expertise, perspective and voice, consider who is best positioned to be impacted by that thought leadership.

Who do you want to reach? What is the underlying message in your thought leadership and how can it benefit others?

Equipped with the answers to these questions, entrepreneurs can begin to formulate an overall plan to leverage their thought leadership for increased influence and visibility. A thought leadership distribution strategy will enable you to create opportunities for targeted business growth.

I help entrepreneurs create custom thought leadership plans that are aligned with the mission and purpose that drives their business. To begin drafting a plan for your thought leadership efforts consider these elements:

- **Subjects** I can speak and write about
- **Audiences** that know me and audiences I want to reach
- **Distribution** channels I will use to convey my thought leadership
- **Outcomes** I am looking for from my thought leadership

Amplify Your Thought Leadership in Others' Presence

You may feel as if you are just one small voice in a big entrepreneurial expertise arena, but the world needs your perspective, opinion and voice. Even on those days when you feel your voice is just a flicker, it has all the elements to ignite a really engaged conversation, dialogue, or discussion. And when it matches up with someone else's ember of thought leadership in conversation, it really fans the flames.

So, who in your circle can echo your thought leadership? Is there someone on social media who you can amplify what they are writing about and add value to their audience?

THOUGHT LEADERSHIP LEADS TO VISIBILITY

Thought leadership can be used as a springboard to position your business for success in year one and beyond. Regardless of where you want your thought leadership to take you, it only takes one ingredient to get started, and that's trust.

- Trust in yourself
- Trust in your expertise
- Trust that you have something to share
- Trust that someone needs to hear what you have to say in the way that only you can say it
- Trust that your perspective is missing in the trending conversations out there.

Your thought leadership will expand as your business grows. Where do you want it to take you and those that you influence?

KEY TAKEAWAYS

- Thought leadership doesn't work without the right mindset: what can you say to silence the voice in your head that claims you are not a thought leader?

- Thought leadership is meant to be shared: how can you become a little more vulnerable and share a little more of you?
- Thought leadership is an extension of your brand: does your brand message support you as a thought leader?

Design Magnetic Marketing
that Fits You
Kate Varness

EVER BEEN TO A WEDDING WHERE THE BRIDESMAIDS WEAR matching dresses and only one of them looks good while the others deal with bulging, bunching and the misery of frumpery?

Marketing your coaching or consulting business is kind of like that: one style doesn't fit all. At the beginning of your business journey, you're likely to defer to expert formulas.

Linda, a coach for empty nesters, was taught to grow her network by sending direct messages to anyone who had "empty nester" in their Facebook bio. Linda hated cold messaging, but she felt obligated to get her money's worth from the program.

Can you guess what happened with Linda? No return on investment, plus she felt guilty for not following the formula. To ease her pain, she told herself the beautiful lie that "someday she would go back to finish the program."

Many new business owners become serial purchasers of courses and programs. They hop from formula to formula until they mistrust their ability to make good buying choices. That means they stop investing even though their marketing problem isn't solved.

Did Linda ever question her assumption of shoving herself into a one-size-fits-all formula? Not really. At least not until we started working together. I showed Linda how custom-tailored marketing strategies made all the difference. Here's what made that possible:

I use a powerful tool called Human Design. In 1987, a man named Ra Uru Hu synthesized Western Astrology, the I Ching, the Kabbalah, the Chakra system, and Quantum Physics into the complex and utterly fascinating Human Design system. He called it "a concrete map to the nature of being." I think of it like an X-ray of an individual's energetic grid.

Your energetic grid influences marketing more than you'd expect. In the beginning stages of a business, you feel pressure to push yourself and do everything quickly. When you're in the frequency of pressure, not good enough or never done, you repel (not attract) ideal clients. Your audience senses when you're out of alignment, which means you can't "fake it till you make it." Linda tried to overcome her dislike of cold messaging tactics and it didn't work.

I wish I had known earlier that I didn't have to force icky formulas, like the bridesmaid stuffing herself into an ill-fitting dress. An alternate path would have looked like this. First, one-to-one Human Design coaching to confirm my natural talents and tendencies, increase my confidence and differentiate my message. After that I'd match up with marketing strategies. Instead, I did things the hard way.

Magnetic marketing depends on knowing your innate talents and tendencies. When you try to skip the step of self-knowledge and simply rely on formulas, your audience senses the gap. They don't pay attention or buy, which leads you to blame the technique or yourself. Instead of having abundance, you slip into lack, not enough time, not enough clients, pressure to lower your price or you over-give. This further repels clients and leads to frustration, anger and bitterness in you.

I guarantee that you have something amazing to offer based on your unique combination of life experiences, talents, skills and perspectives. Start there. Use Human Design to confirm what you already know about yourself and to highlight the value only you can bring.

In addition to strengthening your self-knowledge, Human Design helps you release the self-doubt that comes from societal conditioning (the rules about what you should and shouldn't do). An example of conditioning in marketing is that you should directly initiate the sale. From the lens of Human Design, only Manifestor Types are aligned with this direct approach. The other 92% try to directly initiate sales without success.

If you're wondering, "Why isn't this working for me?" then it's time to find marketing methods that match your unique energy grid, rather than force a formula. Each Human Design Type has a different strategy to align with their energy flow. Check my bio for how to get your free Human Design chart.

Manifestors (8% of the population) initiate things through an independent, non-verbal creative flow. Their strategy is to inform the people who will be impacted by their actions so that everyone is on the same page and to minimize interruptions. Manifestors get angry when their process is interrupted because they may not be able to rejoin the creative flow. Keeping others in the loop lessens resistance and ensures a more peaceful process.

Generator and Manifesting Generator Types (70% of the population) bring ideas into form. They are not meant to directly initiate. Their strategy is to wait to respond. When they are asked to do something, Generators need to pause and answer this question: "Do I have energy to do this?" Just because they can do the work doesn't mean they should do it. Generators also need to wait to respond to new ideas. Not every inspiration should be acted upon. Generators thrive when they take time to play with ideas and notice what shows up in their field of awareness before moving forward.

Projectors (21% of the population) provide wise guidance, but they have to wait to be invited to share their insights. When they don't follow this strategy, they feel bitter that people don't value what they're saying. Projectors yearn to be acknowledged by others. Recognition doesn't come from being the loudest person in the room. It happens when Projectors learn how to ask questions that may lead to an invitation, to use silence and to passionately talk about what they do.

Reflectors (1%) have an energetic flow tied to the lunar cycle. Their strategy is to wait a full cycle of the moon before responding to important decisions. Reflectors play a vital role in helping us see the health of an organization or community. The open design of Reflectors means they hold up a mirror so others can see themselves and gain powerful self-knowledge. Reflectors need to give themselves permission to take as long as necessary in decision-making.

Each of these strategies is very different. You become a magnetic marketer when you have the self-knowledge that comes from Human Design. Listed below are Type-specific ways for you to let go of "shoulds" and affirm your natural energetic path. Notice which beliefs are getting in your way and use the trust statements to nurture your confidence.

MANIFESTORS – THE INITIATORS

Areas of conditioning and self-doubt:

- I should be the one who finishes all projects, not just starts them
- People won't like it if I am direct.

Trust your powerful design:

- I reduce resistance when I inform others who may be impacted
- I'm not asking permission or forgiveness, only giving others a heads up
- It's okay to tell a particular person that my offer may be a good match.

Generators – The Builders

Areas of conditioning and self-doubt:

- If I'm capable of doing something that I'm asked to do, I should do it
- Frustration is a sign that I'm failing.

Trust your powerful design:

- My natural flow is to respond to life. When I show up and do what I love, it starts a conversation and that gives me something more to respond to
- I ask my Sacral if I have energy for a task before I do it
- I look for ways to have conversations with potential clients. I enjoy getting to know them.

Manifesting Generators – The Express Builders

Areas of conditioning and self-doubt:

- I have to pick a niche to be successful
- I need to make things happen.

Trust your powerful design:

- I am a genius at finding shortcuts. I love moving fast
- It's vital for me to have multiple things going on at the same time because it helps me use up my excess energy. I don't have to finish them all
- I sparkle when I am excited about something, and people notice that.

Projectors – The Guides
Areas of conditioning and self-doubt:

- If I just push through now, I will be able to rest later
- My business needs to be visible everywhere or I'll miss opportunities.

Trust your powerful design:

- When I rest and restore my body, spirit and mind, I make more money. It's correct for me to receive support
- I love presenting at summits, on podcasts or being asked for guidance. These opportunities come to me when I am out in the world
- I carry myself like a Queen. I never give unsolicited advice.

Reflectors – The Assessors
Areas of conditioning and self-doubt:

- I need to hurry up and decide
- It's my job to fix others, even when they disappoint me.

Trust your powerful design:

- I instinctively sense someone's potential and am aware of the potential for humanity, too
- My health depends on being in the right place with the right people

- Through me, others can see a mirror of themselves. I don't need to fix them; My presence alone brings them great value.

Having insight into your Human Design lets you release the conditioning that tells you to fix yourself and to choose marketing strategies that match who you really are. Just like someone sashaying down an aisle in a custom-made dress, you will magnetically attract clients to your unique offer.

KEY TAKEAWAYS

- Magnetic marketing starts with self-knowledge, not formulas.
- Notice when you're forcing and proving. These are signs of conditioning to release.
- Forgive your "buying mistakes" along the way. Cut your losses, then invest in one-to-one help.
- Remember that you have powerful gifts to share with the world. You don't need to be fixed. You are naturally creative, resourceful and whole. Let your light shine.

Part Four
LIFESTYLE

Boundaries

Margaret Martin

ONE OF THE THINGS AN ENTREPRENEUR MUST DO IS LEARN HOW and when to set boundaries. It is very important, and if you are working from home, it is a must. If setting boundaries is hard for you, perhaps this chapter will provide guidance and comfort.

What is a boundary? A boundary is, just as it sounds, a protection line, invisible fence or bubble you imagine around you to protect you from the words and/or actions of others. Boundaries help you define who you are, your character, your values and who you are not. It is like a moat around a castle, to protect and establish a safe distance from other people's intrusion, harm or negativity.

Boundaries are so essential that a lack of them can affect all aspects of your business. For example, my client Barbara came to my coaching program with the goal of being more productive. Through our sessions I discovered she needed to set a boundary with her mother. Barbara's mother did not drive and needed my client to take her to her appointments and errands, and her mother would schedule them in the middle of the client's workday.

Barbara was exasperated and becoming resentful of her mother, thinking that she was being selfish and not caring about her business.

We worked together to develop some language to explain to her mother that she would schedule days and times for her appointment and errands. Her mother was hurt and angry at first, but with my client's patience, firm boundaries and clear communication, they were able to take a somewhat volatile situation and turned it into a win-win for both of them. It took several weeks to create the new routines for both of them, and there were sometimes when patience wore thin, yet the outcome was so rewarding. Neither of them lost love or respect for each other.

So, in what areas of your life can you set up boundaries? Following are my suggestions.

YOUR SCHEDULE

Depending on your personal situation (single, married, children, parents, pets), it may be that your schedule might vary from day to day. Get it mapped out as firmly as you can, then be flexible when the shifts happen. For me, I have an established routine for my day: early morning routine, get into my office by 9:00 a.m., appointments start at 10:00 a.m., and I work until between 5:00 or 6:00 p.m. Yes, situations come up that require that I change my schedule. But in certain circumstances, I cannot be flexible and accommodate the interruption because of my boundaries around client work.

MINIMIZE DISTRACTIONS

Working from home requires focus and not being distracted by the things you see that need to be done – no chores during your working hours or children interrupting "just because."

RESPONDING TO EMAILS

I suggest never or at least limited response to emails on the weekend or after 8:00 p.m. Responding at any time of day/night over the weekend sets you up for being available 24/7. When you make yourself available to your clients at all hours of the day and night, many will take advantage of you and expect to hear from you immediately, thus setting up a situation of burnout, feeling unappreciated and exhaustion. It's rare when I answer emails on the weekend or late evenings, and it must be in response to a client's important question.

Determine what boundaries you want to set and realize that with each one there may be a consequence and a reaction to the boundary. Then let people know what the boundaries are, so they can be prepared when they overstep it.

For example, if you are working from home, you will need to advise your children that when the door to your office is closed, they may not enter unless it is an emergency. I would suggest that you explain what constitutes an emergency and put it in writing and post on your door, so it is easily seen.

When you need to set a boundary with someone, here are some simple steps you can take:

1. Set the boundary and advise them
2. Advise them when they cross your boundary
3. Warn them again
4. Take your action

For instance, let's say you are talking on the phone with someone, and suddenly they change their tone and start criticizing you. Instead of reacting and defending yourself, at that point you set your boundary: (1) "I want to let you know that I am not going to be talked to like that by you or anyone else." (2) Then say, "You are talking to me in a manner that is unacceptable and if you continue (3) I will hang up the phone." Then if they continue (4) you would say, "I am hanging up the phone now." And do it!

Should they call you back, you have the choice of answering the phone and saying, "Are you willing to talk to me in a manner that is more appropriate? If not, I will hang up again." Or don't answer the phone. A point to note: some people will go to great lengths to try to get to you. If they cannot reach you by phone, they may resort to emails or letters. At least by email, you can block them, and if letters come, you can choose not to read them or have someone else read them and tell you if there is anything of importance in them.

Put your needs and your self-care ahead of anyone else's needs, and you must be willing to live with the consequences and their reaction to your stand. As Brené Browns says, "Daring to set boundaries is about *having the courage to love ourselves, even when we risk disappointing others.*" There is almost always pushback, at least initially. Often people are hesitant to enforce their boundaries because they fear losing the friend, acquaintance, business deal or opportunity. Or he or she may be afraid of an overreaction or possible harm from the person with whom they are setting the boundary.

If you are hesitant to take this action, you may be in avoidance or fear, and you may already be suffering a huge consequence by not enforcing your boundary. This person is sucking the life out of you. I'm pretty sure that is not what you want. If what you want is to be honored and respected, then do what it takes to take care of yourself.

In some cases, you may hesitate to set boundaries because you feel unworthy or perhaps have low self-confidence. It does take a lot of courage to make this choice but know that *you are worth it,* and you will be supported!

People will treat you as you allow them. Take good care of yourself, insist that all people treat you well.

This may sound counter intuitive, people treating us as we allow, yet it is the case. We grow up modeling behaviors of our parents and other role models. Rarely is there an example of someone advising you that you really are in charge of your life and to set standards to be treated well.

You have the opportunity now to change things. Take responsibility for you, own your power and guide others as to how you would like to be treated. That is what setting boundaries is about.

A few additional tips for setting boundaries:

- Be respectful when setting a boundary
- Plan your response for when someone crosses the boundary
- Someone's feelings may be hurt yet remember you cannot control how other people feel.

When you take the time to honor yourself and set boundaries around yourself with people, schedules and other's expectations, you will lead a much happier life. You will be less stressed, have improved relationships, more respect from others, and more than likely, you will have less conflict in your life.

It may take some time and be a bit of a rocky road at times, but keep the faith and be persistent, you will be glad you did. Remember, you and you alone choses who and how you want to be in the world. Own your power and show up for your life. You've got this!

KEY TAKEAWAYS

- Setting boundaries is one of the keys to having a happy life
- When you set boundaries with others, you increase your self-respect
- You will be much more productive when you set boundaries
- Self-care is one of the results of setting boundaries
- When you set boundaries, you tell others how you want to be treated.

How to Succeed in Business without Sabotaging Your Health
Maureen "Mo" Cooper

You know the song, "It's a Man's World?" Yeah, right! Women have gone from martini makers to breadwinners, while juggling family, career, household, kids, pets, meals, shopping and the emotional well-being of everyone around us. And the thing that suffers at the end of the day is our health. And if your health is suffering, eventually everything will suffer!

"Hold on. You have no idea what I'm going through! I'm running a business! It's non-stop chaos on a stick! How am I supposed to juggle a personal life *and* a business *and* focus on my health? Who do you think I am: Superwoman?!"

You don't have to be Superwoman. Superwoman comes from another planet; you're here, knee-deep in laundry, Zoom calls and cooking. But like superheroes, we all need to prioritize for success. Superheroes have it easy; they know it's their job to save the planet. You don't hear them saying: "I don't have time to save the planet! I've got laundry to do!" Their priority is to protect us from life's perils. Funnily enough, that's our main job too: to protect ourselves from life's perils, even if we still have to do the dang laundry! Taking a page from the superhero notebook, it's time to prioritize our well-being.

We invest time every day. However, we often don't actually know how we're investing our time. That's crazy since well-used time is like magic! Intentionally spent time determines what we accomplish, the amount of stress we have, our level of health, how well we love, mental clarity and sleep quality. This is great news!

Humans are wired for rewards. Why you do something has to be meaningful! My "why" came gradually. In 1999, I woke on a frigid November morning in Canada, and the left side of my body wasn't moving as fast as the right. An MRI confirmed it was Multiple Sclerosis (MS). Did I start living a healthy life then? Nope! A couple of weeks of recovery and back to work and single parenting I went!

Then, I got married, had another baby, moved away from my family to another country, and relapsed. Did I get healthy then? Heck no, I had kids to raise and a house to run. Then, at thirty-six, it hit me: if I wanted another baby, it had to happen immediately!

Ten months later, our "little" baby girl rocked our world! Imagine my surprise when she weighed a scant nine-and-a-half pounds and not the sixty-five pounds I had gained! That *still* wasn't reason enough to weave health into my busy schedule. I just had a baby! With two boys and a baby in tow, an exhausting marriage, and endless volunteer commitments, there just wasn't time. Then it happened.

On Christmas 2008, my then-husband handed me a present with the disclaimer, "It's only because you said you wanted to get into shape!"

My gift was a Wii game called EA Sports Personal Trainer. I reluctantly tried it. I liked it! It was kind of fun! But when was I going to fit it in? The time had come. Time to put my health first. But... how?

The only time of day I had to do anything for myself was early morning. Five in the morning was my new normal, working out four times a week. It was so peaceful that I started getting up early every day. I would read, journal or simply enjoy my coffee in solitude – time just for me!

Over the next few years, I began to weave healthy practices into my everyday life. I joined a gym and a running club to surround myself with healthy, like-minded people. I hired a personal trainer. I soon realized living a message of health was my calling and became a personal trainer and a nutrition coach. I ran a successful bootcamp for two-and-a-half years, encouraging thousands to live healthier lives.

It was fulfilling, but it was a grind. At forty-six years old, I ran ten outdoor boot camps a week; three of them were at 4:45 a.m.! If I didn't get a handle on my schedule, I was going to relapse, fail at my business and not be there for my family or my clients. Thus, my non-negotiable pillars of health were born. I wanted to thrive, not just survive! That is my "why" I do what I do every single day.

My non-negotiable practices are based on five areas of health: mindset and time management, nutrition, spiritual/emotional care, movement and rest and recovery (sleep!). These pillars provide essential health support so the rest of the day can flow easily around them.

Mindset and Time Management is the first and foundational pillar. Like Maslow's Hierarchy of Needs, this pillar is the foundation of all health. Maslow's base layer is physiological needs (food and clothing). These are non-negotiables we need to grow and thrive. Creating a solid foundation of non-negotiables of healthy practices allows you to accomplish more in less time, have more flow in your every-day life, and notice more joy! Sound business practice is setting business hours. Stay within your hours as much as possible. You will gain notoriety as someone who prioritizes, and less availability boosts your time value. Not to mention freeing you up to do the things you want.

Pillar two is feedbag time! Nutrition is the cornerstone of health. "Let food be thy medicine and medicine be thy food," said Hippocrates. But, eating healthy is a pain in the behind and there are many mixed messages about what *is* "healthy." The easiest path to eating healthier is to stick to "real food" 85% of the time. "Real food" is vegetables, lean meats, and fresh fruits –mainly items on the outside perimeter of your grocery store. The less you shop the center aisles, the better. Healthy eating creates a profound shift; you may move better, have fewer pains, reduce medications, lower weight, have clearer thinking, better stress management and more energy. Wow!

Speaking of stress, pillar three is Spiritual and Emotional Care. Have you ever tried to make a sound decision while completely stressed out? Do you even know you're stressed out? Do you say, "Busy!" when people ask how you are? Stress interferes with productivity, mental clarity, sound decision-making and physical well-being. First thing in the morning, read something uplifting for five minutes to create clarity in your day. Practice three to five minutes of breathing techniques while heading into work or waiting for a Zoom meeting to begin. Calming the nervous system will prepare you mentally. Going for a walk, reading something inspirational or just stopping to mindfully breathe can reset the brain to better handle stressors. Regulating stress hormones allows you to let go of unnecessary weight: both literally and figuratively.

Time to get a move on! So many are chained to desks with virtual work conditions. The fourth pillar is Movement. Implementing movement throughout the day is important because sitting has become the new smoking. A myriad of health issues is associated with prolonged sitting: decreased oxygen, increased blood pressure, joint pain, headaches, chronic fatigue and varicose veins, just to name a few. Using the Pomodoro Productivity Technique works wonders to get up and move around every twenty-five minutes with a longer break every ninety minutes. Stuck in a long meeting? Use Pomodoro to do stretches right at your desk! Ankle rolls, leg extensions, sitting up straight; keep moving to increase blood flow and stay alert. A little goes a long way!

The fifth and most important pillar is Rest and Recovery (Sleep!). If your attitude is "I'll sleep when I'm dead," you'll likely prove that sooner than later! We all have unique sleep needs but feeling rested is going to affect your business productivity, decision making, energy and communication. Set a steady bedtime every night (non-negotiable!). That Netflix series will be there tomorrow. Go to bed. Create a wind-down routine to prepare the body for slumber. Dim lights, soft music, warm shower; whatever it takes to tell your body it's time to rest and everything not done yet can wait for tomorrow.

If this seems overwhelming, don't worry; you're not alone! Meaningful change takes time. Choose one thing to focus on at a time. Something you are ready, willing and able to do. The more sustainable, the more successful you'll feel. That's a great foundation upon which to build more healthy habits. If you need more help, consult a coach, a trainer, a mentor, a therapist (I'm the poster child for therapy!) or enlist a healthy-minded friend to guide you. Investing in a healthy lifestyle will give you more success than any financial investment you'll ever make. So, what are you investing in? Time. Invest a small amount of time in these pillars in your calendar to start. The following are some practices you can do right now to start implementing healthy practices into your day!

Key Takeaways

- **Mindset and Time Management**. Do a time audit of a typical day to see where and how you are investing your time. Select one practice you'd like to start initiating and put it on your calendar as a non-negotiable daily gift to give yourself. Tightening up your work times will give you more urgency to get things done. Deadlines work!
- **Nutrition**. Here's an easy starter: put a glass of water on your bedside table and drink it as soon as you get up to start your day hydrated. Schedule your dinners and time for meal planning. You'll be happy you did! Less chaos

means more productivity in your business and more time for fun!

- **Emotional/Spiritual Care**. Start each day with a simple two-to-three-minute breathing practice. There are numerous free version apps you can use. Calm, Headspace, Mental. These resources have guidelines to incorporate breathing practice and meditation into your daily life for better mental clarity and lower stress.
- **Movement**. Set a twenty-five-minute timer while you work. When the timer rings, get up and move for five minutes! Get more water, send a message to a loved one, make your bed (if you're home). This physical movement and mental break will give you just enough time and space to return to work refreshed.
- **Rest and Recovery (Sleep!)**. Setting up an evening routine to wind down, especially through the workweek, will pay off in better productivity, clarity, choices, and overall well-being throughout the day! A rested mind gets more done and done well.

Don't Let Your Body
Shut Down Your Business
Kelly Lutman

As my eyes scanned the buzzing room of business networkers, I caught sight of a woman I had seen a few times recently. This woman, who had exuded passion in the past, seemed deflated. She looked up cautiously and caught my eye, then slowly moved my way.

"Sharon," I said softly when she was close enough to hear. "Are you okay?"

"Not exactly. Can we talk?" She motioned to two chairs in a quiet corner.

"What's up?" I asked as she slumped into her chair.

"I'm struggling. My body seems to have gone on strike and checked out of participating in my business. I can get a couple hours of effective work in the morning—once I finally wake up—and then hit a wall in the afternoon. I've read your recent blog posts and I know the canned energy drinks I'm using are just a crutch. My business was just beginning to have traction and grow, but now I can barely keep up!"

"Sounds like you could nap several times a day. Are you sleeping well at night?" I asked. "Do you struggle to shut down your monkey mind to get to sleep, or maybe get back to sleep after waking to pee?"

"Yeah, that monkey mind was often an issue as I first started business, and I often got up to work in the wee hours of the night. Now I can sleep for hours and feel like I just had a short nap. I can barely wake up without a couple cups of strong coffee."

"Sharon," I asked, leaning in a little. "Did you consider yourself healthy when you started your business?"

She nodded, seeming perplexed by my question. "I still think I'm healthy, just really tired from all the demands of getting the business off the ground. Can you recommend something to take? There are so many options available."

I smiled. It was quite common for people to consider themselves healthy, despite a few nagging symptoms. Like Sharon, they often sought answers to symptoms rather than seeing their symptoms as their bodies' cries for help.

We talked about her normal work pattern before the fatigue set in, and I wasn't surprised to hear that she worked long hours to promote her business. As her passion drove her focus, she forgot to take care of herself and her body, a key player in an entrepreneur's business, suffered the results.

I explained the key foundational steps I guide my clients through to support their bodies for better function. These are upgrading food, optimizing digestion, hydrating, moderating stress, prioritizing sleep, and cultivating a positive mindset. Let me share these with you as well.

Our culture and popular media have taught us to choose our food based on taste and convenience, rather than considering what best fuels our body for proper function. You see, food is more than an appetizing experience; it provides information and building blocks for our bodies.

Processed foods that are prominent in grocery stores and restaurants have been manipulated with chemicals and ingredients to extend their shelf life and even promote an addictive effect on us. They provide the wrong information and, sadly, minimal nutrient building blocks.

I strongly recommend that you seek food that is closest to the way it grew and is perishable. These are mostly found on the outer perimeter of the grocery store. Eating the colors of the rainbow in food rather than its packaging will give you a wide array of nutrients for your body to use.

Skip the added sugar and artificial sweeteners, since these are part of the addictive action of processed food and they suppress your immune system for up to four hours after consumption. If you find this challenging, raw local honey, monk fruit, and stevia can provide sweetening that doesn't work against you.

I also recommend an oil change, shifting to using extra virgin olive oil or coconut oil in place of the corn and vegetable oils that damage cell membranes and hinder their function.

Once you have upgraded your food, you will want to ensure that your body is using it effectively by optimizing your digestion. Step one is to actually sit down and focus on your food without work distractions. Step two is to chew—a lot. I'm not referring to chomp, chomp, swallow, but rather chewing five, ten maybe fifteen times per bite before you swallow.

Why so many times? Because chewing is both a mechanical and chemical part of digestion—and the only part that you have control over, I might add. As you chew, your teeth break down the food and your saliva mixes in enzymes to begin the digestive process before the food enters your stomach.

If you experience acid reflux or GERD, it is a sign that your body isn't able to digest protein well. In fact, the pain you experience in your upper chest or throat is not because you have too much stomach acid, but decades of studies have shown that there is too little. The lower esophageal sphincter becomes floppy when the stomach acidity is reduced and allows stomach acid to burble up into the esophagus.

It burns because your esophagus lacks the mucosal lining of the stomach! I encourage you to not simply pop a pill to make it feel better but to get help with identifying the root cause and correcting it for long-term benefit.

Lastly, you should eliminate solid waste at least once daily. If not, it's a sign that your digestion is not working properly, and your body is reabsorbing toxins it was trying to expel. Yuck! Eating more vegetables and increasing your water consumption can help with elimination, as can taking a probiotic.

Speaking of water, how much do you drink each day? Our bodies are estimated to be seventy percent water so hydration is vital for proper organ function and nutrient dissemination. Drinking plenty of water also supports the function of our lymph system, which transports immune cells around the body and collects waste for elimination.

The majority of your liquid consumption should be filtered plain or infused water, or herbal tea. I recommend filtering your water because the chlorine and fluoride so common in our water supply can hinder absorption of iodine that is vital for proper thyroid function and good metabolism. I also suggest a filter on your shower head as the heat of the water creates steam which distributes chlorine in a way that is absorbed faster in your body.

We can't realistically eliminate stress from our lives, but there are ways to moderate its effect on our bodies. When you are revved up with a busy schedule and running from one thing to the next, your body is in "fight or flight" mode, and it favors the body systems which support escape, while shutting down digestive and reproductive systems. A meal eaten on the run is not well digested.

One of the simplest ways to cool the physiological fire of "fight or flight" is to stop, close your eyes, and breathe deeply. Just five minutes several times a day of slowly breathing in through your nose and out through your mouth will lower your heart rate and calm your body. You could combine this with meditation. If you are new to meditation, I recommend using a guided meditation app to start.

Not only will breathing and meditation calm the flurry inside, but it will also put you into "rest and digest" mode that supports better digestion. Your body will support your big plans when you give it the breaks to relax and digest the food you eat.

I believe the old phrase that "sleep is overrated" was coined by a person who wasn't healthy or was trying to push others to meet an unrealistic agenda. Sleep is vital for proper function. Those with a long to-do list think that sleep is wasted time because they aren't checking things off the list. Yet without sleep, their body isn't able to rejuvenate to complete their list!

The liver and immune system are particularly busy at night, along with hormones being balanced, and the brain processing memories. In fact, if you have a complex decision to make or problem to solve, you would do well to "sleep on it." Review what you know about the situation before you go to bed, and while you sleep, your brain will work on it and you may wake to a clear answer. Far better to sleep rather than pull an all-nighter!

While Sharon wasn't in the frame of mind to tackle all of these as once, I coached her through small, sustainable steps and she gradually emerged from her fog. She blocked time each day to care for herself and no longer worked late at night. An exciting step for her was to delegate some of her tasks to others and focus her own efforts on the aspects of her business for which she was uniquely equipped.

If you are on a path similar to Sharon's, I encourage you to listen to your body and prioritize incorporating these key areas of support to ensure that your body is able to carry you on the entrepreneurial path of your vision. Recognize that health is wealth, and you will have a firm foundation from which to soar in business.

KEY TAKEAWAYS:

- Shop the perimeter of the grocery store for fresh, organic foods free of additives and preservatives.

- Your dis-ease is providing you with important information that you can use to improve your health.
- Get good sleep, drink lots of water, and move your body to stay healthy!

Anyone can be an Ecopreneur
Orianna Nienan

Natural goods have always been on my radar, but I *really* got into natural products in 2008 when I was pregnant with my son. I avoided produce on the "dirty dozen" list, and I paid more attention to what I was putting in and on my body. I took a prenatal docosa-hexaenoic acid (DHA) supplement and ate recommended "brain foods" like walnuts. Slowly, I started to replace products in my home. I stopped using dryer sheets and made DIY wool dryer balls. I read about the chemicals in toothpaste and deodorant, and started making my own.

Did my love of natural products seep into my professional life at first? Not exactly. At that time, I was a management consultant, selling and delivering software and IT services to the government. My life toggled "both worlds." On any day, I could be consulting in a high-rise office in Washington, D.C., and then driving to New Jersey to go primitive camping with a naturalist and learn about plant medicine.

I mention this because being an ecopreneur doesn't mean you have to be a non-corporate type. Ecopreneurship means being concerned about the environment and adopting eco-friendly business practices. It also doesn't mean that we must change who we are or what we look like —unless we want to, of course.

In other words, if you're an entrepreneur, you can be an ecopreneur—*no matter what business you're in.*

While I still provide corporate management consulting services, I did figure out a way to merge my traditional business skills with my Earth-friendly values. I started an eCommerce business called Product Love, whose mission is to educate others about healthy living, connect people with environmentally responsible products and brands and advocate for the Earth. Rather than only focusing on the ethos of "buy less," I promote the message to "buy smart." We're humans and we consume things. I don't expect the general population to stop buying lipstick. However, we can also bring awareness to our choices and the impact we have on the natural world.

Over the past ten years, I have been one of the many people pioneering the ecopreneur movement. I've learned through trial and error. I have helped shape products as a consumer through what I buy and the feedback I provide to brands. With Product Love, I've gotten into eco-production details as we develop our first in-house environmentally responsible products. Based on my experience, here are four suggestions on how you can align your work with eco-friendly practices and embody the new ecopreneur.

DEFINE YOUR BUSINESS VISION, MISSION AND VALUES

This is good advice for any new entrepreneur, however in this case, specifically consider how your business impacts the environment. Do you have a brick-and-mortar facility? Do you produce products? Are you an online-only services business? These scenarios present different opportunities for crafting your vision, mission and values with a focus on sustainability. In terms of specific wording, this could be as simple as including sustainability as a business value.

As an example, here are Product Love's vision, mission and values statements:

- **Vision:** Product Love envisions a world where it is easy to access healthy, sustainable, responsible products. Rather than advocate for more regulation, we see an opportunity to educate and inspire change at the grassroots level.
- **Mission:** Our mission is to educate others about healthy living, connect people with environmentally responsible products and brands, and advocate for the Earth.
- **Values:** Humans are part of multiple large ecosystems and have a responsibility to every other participant in those ecosystems. Our work centers on the values of respecting Nature and recognizing the beauty of creation.

PRODUCT LOVE IS AN ECO-FORWARD eCOMMERCE BUSINESS, BUT what if you're an online life coach and deliver services virtually? How can you incorporate environmentally focused values into your business?

Coaches come in a myriad of flavors, but most provide a self-assessment tool of some sort. A coach could decide on a mission or value of *"helping people live their healthiest life."* Based on this mission, part of the initial coaching self-assessment tool could include a section on non-toxic products and bringing awareness to the health benefits of removing certain chemicals from the home. As you can see from this example, you don't even need to use the words "green," "sustainability," or "eco-friendly" in your vision, mission and values statements to consider yourself an ecopreneur!

SIGN UP FOR A GREEN BUSINESS BUREAU (GBB) MEMBERSHIP

I understand that when you're just starting out, prioritizing business expenses is a must. However, if you are still working on the fundamentals of setting up your business, you may find joining the GBB and completing their EcoAssessment™ helpful. Depending on your answers, you may be able to achieve a GBB certification and include their logos on your business website. Depending on your typical customer avatar, this could be a great selling point and create trust with potential buyers of your products or services. A GBB membership also includes an EcoProfile of your business which may assist in marketing efforts.

The EcoAssessment™ will make you think about obvious and non-obvious ways to consider instilling sustainability into your business. This could be anything from installing recycle bins in your physical store to printing fewer documents in your home office.

CONSIDER YOUR PRODUCT DESIGN, MATERIALS SOURCES, Packaging and Distribution Channels

There is a huge opportunity for entrepreneurs who are focused on creating physical products to effect environmental change. Types of things to consider include:

- How much plastic is included in my product design and packaging?
- What chemicals are included in my product?
- Is my product recyclable?
- What are sources for eco-friendly packaging?
- How long will my product be in a landfill after my customer throws it away?
- Where are my goods being produced and what is the environmental impact of shipping?
- What are the environmental practices of suppliers and other companies I am working with?

ONCE YOU START ANSWERING THESE QUESTIONS, YOU MAY START to see limitations in available solutions. Depending on your business plan and available resources, you may need to start out with the best available solution and then craft a plan to shift your production over time.

One business story I find inspirational is the beauty brand Pyt. On Pyt's "About Us" page, it says: *"We Are Clean: Product, Performance, Planet, Conscience."* (I just love this!) The Pyt brand was started by Amy Carr and Mary Schulman, friends who had a new vision of make-up.

In an interview for their University of Maryland alumni newsletter, the pair were asked to share their "fearless idea." They responded, "To provide clean beauty products at a reasonable price for all who seek it...we really want to change the makeup of makeup. We want ingredients that are not only good for you but also good for our planet. We want packaging that won't just end up in landfills but rather be recyclable or made from recyclable plastic. We want to move the industry forward." It took them several years to develop product formulas and packaging, but their brand is free of thirty plus ingredients that have been determined harmful to human health and they have made big strides in better plastic solutions. Their story helps me to remember that new ways of producing are possible!

CONSIDER ESTABLISHING AN ENVIRONMENTALLY FOCUSED Giving Plan

If you love the idea of being an ecopreneur but you're not sure how it applies to your business, perhaps the one thing you can do is to establish a giving program focused on environmental causes. In business, there will be times when we print a whole ream of paper, drive 300 miles for sales calls or choose a less than perfect option for product packaging due to budget constraints. Establishing a program such as giving 1% of your profits to help offset your impact makes anyone an ecopreneur. This applies to coaches, bookkeepers, online marketers, restaurant owners or any other type of entrepreneur you can think of. If this action appeals to you, you may want to consider joining 1% For the Planet, a membership-based organization that advises on giving strategies and certifies annual donations to environmental causes.

There are many wonderful organizations to consider supporting. Do a little research and check the organization's integrity using a tool such as Charity Navigator. Some of my favorites include The Ocean Cleanup, Ocean Conservancy, and The Nature Conservancy.

So, which step will you take first? Now that you know some initial steps such as defining your vision, mission and values statements, joining the GBB, and establishing an environmentally focused giving plan, you are well on your way to becoming an ecopreneur. One of the beauties of designing your own business is that you get to decide what it looks like.

Whatever actions you decide to take, it's a great idea for them to feel authentic rather than forced. Even though I fit the Green Business Bureau's definition of an ecopreneur—"an entrepreneur focused on creating and selling environmentally-friendly products and services"—I think that anyone who considers the environment when developing their business is an ecopreneur at heart. Throw out all the definitions, judgements, and "shoulds," and decide what being an ecopreneur means for you.

KEY TAKEAWAYS

- If you're an entrepreneur, you can be an ecopreneur—*no matter what business you're in.*
- Consider your environmental posture when defining your business vision, mission, and values.
- Signing up for a Green Business Bureau (GBB) membership will give you ideas about how to make your

business more sustainable—and being a member may help in your marketing!

- Entrepreneurs creating physical products have a huge opportunity to reduce their impact by considering product design, materials, packaging, distribution channels and other production elements.
- Establishing an environmentally focused giving plan (which could include joining the 1% For the Planet movement) is an easy way that anyone can be an ecopreneur.
- Throw out any "shoulds" and design your business based on what feels authentic to you.

The COVID Pivot

Gabriela Bocanete

MY DESIRE TO BE A QUALIFIED, HOLISTIC-HEALTH COACH WAS
sparked by my need to understand and remedy the long-term effects
of the major surgeries I've undergone since my early childhood.
Those surgeries, and the resulting consequences to my physical and
mental wellbeing, ignited a voracious curiosity about alternative, non-
invasive and healthful practices such as yoga and using food as
medicine.

But I wasn't always a health coach. In my career as a conference
interpreter, interpreter trainer and speaker, I worked internationally
for many years. My life consisted of periods of intense activity
involving at least one major conference per month, each of which
required extensive travel, a lot of technical documentation reading in
preparation, plenty of research and having to create bilingual
glossaries.

Given the cognitively-demanding and stressful nature of the
profession, it's no wonder I pursued more advanced studies in mind-
body disciplines such as yoga, Qi Gong, meditation and Yoga Nidra.
Whatever helped me to keep balanced and manage my stress-levels, I

passed on to my colleagues, clients and students. That's how I became an expert on stress, and its causes and consequences. And long before the term "resilience" came into our mainstream vocabulary, I had created and delivered a series of three webinars on the topic.

This digital nomad lifestyle, the "sprint" of intense activity followed by downtime and recovery suited me to a tee.

We had built a yoga studio in our back garden, and I was holding weekly yoga and relaxation sessions, as well as doing gong and sound therapy healing. Clients were asking for more video lectures, so I planned and structured an online course that would help them stay calm and balanced in stressful times.

My first online course—Calm, Vitality, Resilience—was ready to launch when COVID brought the world to a standstill. Everyone suddenly felt fearful and there was a lot of confusion. At first, I felt stunned as I watched the news in disbelief. This couldn't be happening. I had so many plans and projects in the pipeline.

Then I perceived a general fear and anxiety, rising by the minute amid the chaos. My instinct was to help people to keep their balance and not become dominated by fear. Whatever their beliefs regarding the virus, the vaccines or the restrictive measures around it all, they needed to be able to stay calm in order to adjust, so they could find a good way through it and make the best decisions for themselves and their families.

My family was also in some kind of shock. Suddenly, we couldn't travel, we couldn't see each other and we had to stay at home except for short walks to buy groceries. Everything got cancelled: conferences, speaking events, trips, meetings and social gatherings. Some people panicked. Most of us believed that normality would resume in a couple of weeks at most. Yet now, as we approach the third anniversary of the pandemic, we're just beginning to return to normal activities.

Reassessing my course, in the light of these new developments, I felt that clients would need much more live time with me, in order to keep their mental balance and wellbeing. They would benefit from my calm presence, and I would tailor the sessions to their specific needs as they arose. It was the only way I could find for them to attain their desired outcomes in such circumstances. Among all the chaos, uncertainty and lack of control, I would create a safe space for them—an oasis of light in the middle of the storm—and together we would help each other stay sane.

This is where the pivot came in.

WHEN I WAS SIX YEARS-OLD, I JOINED A BALLET CLASS, DANCING *pliés*, *rond-de-jambs*, and *port-de-bras*, I learned to pivot and do pirouettes. Little did I know that pivoting would become a much-needed life skill that is so useful in business and moments of crisis.

My online course, with professionally-produced video lectures and plenty of support, already included plenty of information on some of the most effective practices out there. However, with the world at a standstill, and so much anxiety everywhere, I doubled the amount of support I offered and included powerful live, weekly online gong and sound therapy events combined with a few other magic ingredients. My clients needed it, and I was ready to make it happen for them.

So, we pivoted from in-person, in-studio practices, to remote, online sessions, including webinars focusing on gentle movement, Yoga Nidra and gong baths. Like many others at that time, we quickly learned that broadcasting online was fraught with technical difficulties. Gong- and singing bowl-based sound baths demand the highest possible sound quality and a noise-free environment. So, to create the most faithful reproduction of an in-studio experience, we needed the best quality broadcasting solution out there. Laptops needed to be upgraded. Our wi-fi was inadequate. Our garden studio had to be acoustically treated. Professional quality microphones, cabling, sound mixers, sound recorders, audio-computer interfaces, specialist software and video equipment were acquired, tested and professionally set up. Quite a pivot indeed!

After intense research to find the best solutions, we reconfigured the gong studio to become a fully-equipped webcasting studio. New high-speed Ethernet cabling had to be run to the studio, directly from our internet router to provide a stable connection for broadcasting, as the wi-fi was completely inadequate for the task.

We dressed the studio with acoustic blankets (quickly removable as required) to dampen the harsh resonances and excessive reverberations in the room. We bought high-quality, extremely low noise professional microphones and stands from Germany. Then a carefully-arranged set of microphones were connected, using the highest quality cables, to a specialist sound mixer/recorder which also acted as an audio to computer interface.

A new laptop capable for handling the audio, video and broadcasting computing load whilst running absolutely silent was acquired along with various types of software to manage the system. Finally, we purchased a special video camera and connected it to our new laptop to complete the installation. Then we spent hours and hours testing and tweaking to ensure the system could produce the highest quality broadcast, one hundred percent reliably, every time. No expense was spared; only the best quality sound for my clients!

Initially, I was in two minds about holding all the client-sessions online. Health coaching implies a high level of confidentiality and trust, as we often discuss sensitive issues. Bringing my full, undivided attention to the individual client and their needs represented the basis on which they build their progress. Still, with a couple of mindset changes, a powerful presence can be brought to an online session. Sensitive issues can still be tackled in confidence if we both follow a few simple rules of Zoom etiquette. It's those few steps outside your comfort zone that bring the best results.

Pivoting in such a short time was not easy; it required fast thinking and a fair investment, plus specialist technical skills to optimize sound and video feeds for the best possible client experience. My husband's experience as a sound genius and a videographer was invaluable.

Now, after the COVID lockdowns and many online sessions, I can say that the pivot has been a huge success and helped many of my clients navigate that awful time and the stresses and impact on mental health that came with it.

Broadcasting weekly online sessions also allowed people to join from further afield, without the need to travel. It's been convenient for them to find a suitable spot to create their Yoga Nidra "nest" to lie in for the practice. Their partners sometimes join them and, if there are pets in the house, they are always listening. Cats and dogs love the gong frequencies! My regulars tune in from the north of England, France, Belgium, Germany, Slovakia, Argentina, Colombia, and Mexico!

Lately I have started inviting people back into my garden studio —it's such a special treat to be in the same space as my mighty gongs! But I can't imagine ever going back to no online sessions at all, as I'm quite happy with a hybrid business now. I have a combination of private or semi-private in-studio sessions, plus the live online group sessions every week. Those enrolled in longer programs get recordings when they miss the live session.

I feel I'm coming out of such a difficult time with a broader audience, a wider reach and more options for my clients. I am sure that there will be more adjustment and settling in the next few years, but for now I'm established in the modalities that work best for my tribe.

Key Takeaways

- Stay open to doing business in new ways so that when a pivot is required, you can make necessary shifts

- Once you make a pivot, decide what elements you want to keep from both your old and new ways of doing business
- When life turns upside down, don't panic. It's better to just trust that you're being led to something bigger and better.

Part Five

ADVERSITY

Recreating Your Career After a Life Transition

Donna Kendrick

IN THE SUMMER OF 2013, OUR YOUNG FAMILY OF FIVE WAS celebrating our move back home to the Philadelphia area, where we would be close to family after seven years away. I was over the moon with excitement to be back on U.S. soil, for the kids to be speaking English in school and for my husband, Greg to take on a role at work that would enable more family time for us.

By the winter of 2013, I had celebrated my fortieth birthday, experienced widowhood, and led my three young children through their first holiday season without their dad. New Year's Eve 2014 arrived, and I felt like the roller coaster of life I was on was about to take a big drop, while I didn't have my seatbelt on. My biggest fear wasn't handling the drop though; it was how I was going to handle the next uphill climb—figuring out how to financially support my three children.

When we first moved home, I'd begun working at our local public school as a teacher's aide making $17,500 a year. I had given up my career in finance seven years earlier to follow Greg abroad, and he had become the breadwinner. After his transition, it felt like his salary stopped literally before the first pot of coffee was brewed in the payroll office that Monday morning.

I knew I needed to go back to work to make enough money to support my kids. I knew I was smart, educated and savvy, but I also knew I didn't have it in me to recreate my career in that first year, and to be honest, in the second year either. I was sick to my stomach every time I thought about leaving my teacher's aide position, as that job allowed me to put my kids through school. For those first two years, I needed the safety of the familiar.

I'm sure you have heard the term "bright-eyed and bushy tailed?" Well, two years after Greg's death, in the spring of 2015, I woke up feeling just that way. I literally sat up in bed, and took an inventory of where my life was, where I wanted it to be and how relaunching my career was the key to it all. I designed a mental roadmap of how to get there that felt like a session of hyper-speed vision-boarding in the classroom of my brain.

That morning, I grabbed the stack of creamy yellow Post-It notes from my nightstand (available for middle-of-the-night brain-dumping) and wrote my ideas down, peeling and sticking the two-inch-by-two-inch squares on the wall at a frantic pace. I had three sections of stickies on the wall: *Community*—how to help young kids in grief, *Career*—what could I do that fueled my soul and helped me feed my kids, and *Family*—work life balance ideas.

I am a person of action, and after digesting the Post-It brain dump decorating my bedroom wall, I decided to flip my career on its head and begin providing financial advice to families in transition for the widow and widowers whose tomorrow feels totally different than their today. I was inspired by the help my new financial advisor provided me in the first two years after Greg's passing, and by the wisdom our original financial advisor shared with us in 2007 before we moved to Italy.

In 2007, Greg and I purchased a variable universal life insurance policy upon the recommendation of this advisor. And after Greg's death, the proceeds from this policy provided me with the funds I needed to keep my house, and to educate my kids over the coming years. Providing financial advice and education to families in transition was my calling, my new passion and my mission. Now, I just had to figure out how to get there with my heart, soul and finances intact. Here are the steps I followed:

STEP ONE: TALK TO THOSE YOU RESPECT IN THE INDUSTRY

In the weeks after my decision to recreate my career, I sat and shared coffee with many that I admired—my advisor at the time, my previous advisor from 2007, a wealth-management dad I knew from my daughter's lacrosse team, his boss and so on. I asked specific and related questions to each, ranging from their salary, their start in the industry, and what a typical day looked like, to the balance between their family and work life and their goals for retirement. I learned there were many different ways to be paid in the industry and a variety of ways you could be employed as an advisor. I knew I wanted to be independent so I could niche my practice for exactly who I wanted to serve, which meant I would be starting off with zero salary and zero income until I grew my client base.

STEP TWO: FIGURE OUT YOUR FINANCES

If I was going to be self-supporting my family until I could start generating an income from this career, I truly needed to get a grip on the daily living costs for the kids and me. Once I had that number solidly established, I needed to figure out my net worth, and what funds were liquid or not tax-sensitive, so that I could use them to supplement the small pension I was receiving from Greg's benefits. Subtracting the annual cost of daily living from the readily available funds I had in front of me, mapped the picture of how long I could afford to support my family and my new business on savings. Success in two and half years; that was my new goal post.

. . .

Step Three: Make a Plan to Be Competitive in the Industry

Once I identified how I wanted to recreate my career in this new stage of my life, as well as how I was going to afford it, my next step was to understand the education and mentorship I would need to be successful. During my interviews with admired advisors, I asked about their education, internships, designations and so on. I had a degree in business statistics and an MBA, but each of my interviewees had started their financial planning careers in their early twenties, so I had time and experience to make up for. I deduced from those conversations that I wanted to enter the industry and mentor to become a Certified Financial Planner®, so I registered for a year-long education program to earn the designation which I studied for alongside the coursework for my three major licenses. I also collaborated with a company that helped me create a timeline to manage my licensing and provided sponsorship for the tests.

Step Four: Listen to Your Gut Instinct

I felt the momentum of all these decisions rolling like a big ol' snowball down a mountain, and my subconscious brain told me I was creating my own avalanche. I froze in place and ran to the safety of my $17,500 a-year job, thinking I could work and manage my studies and mentoring all at the same time. I was overwhelmed by my frozen confidence, but there was this feeling in my belly, urging me to keep going all-in on this career plan. Yes readers, all through my life I have listened to my belly. When my belly turned sideways, I stopped in my tracks, and in those times when I didn't listen to my belly and went against my intuition, the outcomes were usually less than agreeable (reference winter 2013). So, when the practical part of my brain was running for safety, I decided to follow my gut instinct and take the risk in quitting my teaching job and going full time back to school to follow my calling to be a financial planner.

. . .

STEP FIVE: KNOW YOUR WORTH

For those considering a career change or new job offer in the years straight after sudden, life-changing circumstances, I encourage you to spend a significant amount of time working on your mindset. Appreciate and honor your specific talents and celebrate your ability to earn a great income through your passion. My biggest hurdle in working as a financial advisor for families in transition was charging for my work. I wanted to do good and be liked, so I often discounted my fees. Soon though, I realized my pricing wasn't in line with the industry, and I was working harder to make less money, while spending less time with my kids as a result. I am here to let you borrow the belief I adopted from this experience: you are worth every penny, and I encourage you to charge accordingly.

IN SUMMARY, I HOPE THESE FIVE STEPS HAVE HELPED TO provide you with a path toward recreating your career after you have faced a life transition. I hope my story has helped you a bit toward recognizing your own human capacity for grit, and the glory of creating your own fresh start. And, as my grandmom would say in her goodbyes, "I give you peace, love and a hug to carry you through the day."

Now, go out there and succeed.

KEY TAKEAWAYS

- Even the darkest life events have silver linings—allow yourself to feel the pain and sorrow before opening up to joy and rebirth.
- You can do hard things!
- Opportunities will come knocking—and you get to open the door to live your best life.

When Life Hands You Lemons
Deborah Kevin

IN THE FALL OF 2021, I WAS IN THE MIDST OF TEACHING TWO publishing cohorts, each filled with author-students. I'd just graduated with my master's degree in publishing from Western Colorado University. The Highlander Press publishing production schedule clicked along at a rapid pace with books slated for publication in October and November.

Then it happened.

I found a lump in my right breast, a growth that turned out to be two cancerous tumors requiring immediate surgery. Suddenly, words like cover, fonts, and layout were replaced with biopsies, ports, and unpronounceable drug names. In my naïveté, I believed that I would be healed completely by year-end, ready to return to work full-time in January.

As I shared the news with my Faith Keeper mastermind members, longtime friends, and peers, I quickly became overwhelmed by their generosity.

"Let me host your weekly Write-Ins," said one.

"I can take over your newsletter and social media," offered another.

"We can walk your dog," several people offered.

"I can drive you to your appointments," said my brother.

My husband Rob completely rearranged his schedule to be present at my appointments and half of my treatments (my brother took the other half)—all while readying his New Jersey home for sale and relocating his mother to Maryland where we lived.

And three incredible women volunteered to lead healing circles focused on eradicating the cancer from my body as I underwent a mastectomy, chemotherapy, radiation, and reconstruction surgery.

I looked at my business differently. *What was essential to keep projects moving forward? What could I give up completely? Where could I outsource?* Subconsciously, I knew that the gift of a cancer diagnosis would allow me to be less of a "doer" and more of a leader. Talk about an energetic shift!

I'd long been a "giver" and it became necessary for me to also be a "receiver." Here are the techniques I used to navigate life and business when the unexpected hit:

ACCEPT HELP

Years ago, I read a book by Amanda Owens called *The Power of Receiving,* and it highlighted all the ways I'd unconsciously been repelling abundance by doing it all myself (picture me as a little girl, hands on hips, a look of fierce determination on my face). I worked on accepting support and feeling gratitude, but the amount of support I needed—physically required—going through this healing journey was so much more than I ever thought.

Quite literally, I couldn't do most things by myself, including driving and opening jars or cans. I lost my hair, including eyebrows and eyelashes (yeah, I was pretty much a naked mole rat), lost two toenails, had a rash covering my entire body, and spent a month battling fevers. I had no choice but to quiet my ego and say "yes" to offered assistance.

The abundance of love, support, encouragement, and help that flowed my way kept me focused on all that was going right in my life. I learned that when one allows loved ones to help, we all feel a lot better through the process.

Practice saying "yes" to those who generously offer support and assistance.

DELEGATE

As a solo entrepreneur, it's easy to fall into the trap of doing everything ourselves. During the first years of our business, it's often necessary that we wear all the hats: CEO, marketing director, designer, copywriter, and so forth. When I knew I'd be working part-time for what turned out to be more than a year, I had the opportunity to delegate tasks that weren't mission-sensitive but still needed to be done. Here are the steps I followed to determine what to delegate:

- Identify all non-mission-critical tasks (answering emails, sending video replays, running my Write-Ins, etc.)
- Prioritize those by what must be done, what would be nice to have done, and what isn't necessary to be done.
- Make a wish list of characteristics for the perfect resource(s) to assume these tasks.
- Document your way of doing the "must" and "nice" tasks so that the process is captured and can easily be replicated (Ninja tip: use Zoom to record you doing these tasks and then your apprentice can make a standard operating procedure document from the recording).

Once you have identified the perfect resource(s), set regular follow-up and check-in meetings to ensure the tasks are completed and any questions that arise can be quickly resolved—then vow to not go back to assuming this work once the crisis is over.

.   .   .

PLAN AHEAD

When you're in the throes of building a business, often money can be a worry, and this can be amplified when life goes wonky and off-plan. I'm no financial planner but know that it's crucial to have *at least* three months' worth of living and business expenses set aside for those times when you need to tap into it.

When my diagnosis came in, I immediately panicked. How would I pay my condo fees? Medical expenses? Contractor invoices? How could I take care of my health, the most important asset I have, while honoring my financial commitments?

Fortunately, I had accumulated some savings which came in handy for covering monthly expenses and my business income covered business commitments. I decided to work part-time while recovering from surgery and undergoing chemo and radiation treatments. I prioritized projects and spent focused time dedicated to one project at a time. I was transparent with my clients and contractors, openly sharing my availability and keeping boundaries in place to protect my health and energy.

Brainstorm a list of regular bills you pay and prioritize them. In some cases, you may have to make difficult decisions for what to (temporarily) cut. Here's a short list of things to consider when setting money aside for emergencies:

Personal

- Mortgage, rent, or condo fee payments
- Monthly insurance: auto, home, health
- Groceries
- Utilities: water, gas, electric, internet/cable
- Recurring payments: car, loans, credit cards

Business

- Subcontractors

- Professional services: attorney, bookkeeper
- Taxes

Positive Mindset

We hear all the time how our mindset reflects our lived experience. Early on, I decided that I wanted to have a magical experience. I named my intravenous port a "portkey," which had to be tapped each time by the nursing staff when they de-accessed and saying, "Mischief managed." I invoked Harry Potter by renaming the pharmacy "the apothecary" and my chemo medications "magical elixirs." I requested that the oncology nursing staff follow my lead, which they all did. I think it made an unpleasant experience fun (or at least as fun as it could have been).

I listened to guided meditations and angel healing music. I focused my energy on eating healthy meals, getting enough sleep (which included a daily nap), and I opted to cut my working hours in half. I also walked between three and five miles a day—every day.

Find recordings and meditations that inspire and uplift you and use them daily. Be sure to put your self-care first on the list because you're healing (either physically or emotionally or both). It's an easy trap to fall into to focus all your energy on business—avoid that trap by prioritizing you.

Stay Present

When one receives upending news, it's easy to trundle down the "what happens if" pathway. In truth, staying present and focusing on the task at hand is one of the greatest gifts I've received from this journey. When the medical professionals handed me a two-inch binder filled with my treatment plan, medicine names, and possible side effects, I created a separate "medical appointments" calendar and added the treatment dates to it before sharing it with my support network. I handed the binder off to Rob and asked him to let me know if anything I experienced was normal. That way, I didn't absorb into my brain all the possible side effects, choosing instead to focus on the tasks at hand: one treatment at a time.

I won't say that I was completely successful staying out of *what-ifs-ville*. In fact, just as I wrapped up the first part of my chemo treatments, I stumbled upon an Instagram post about a twelve-old-girl who'd just lost her battle with cancer. The post included a photo of a healthy-looking and vibrant young woman with the tag, "This was taken two weeks ago." My heart dropped and tears that I'd long tamped down burst out in a torrent. How could such a beautiful and effervescent girl go from thriving to dead in such a short time? That knocked me sideways and I may have crawled into bed for a couple of days. I didn't stay down; I leaned into all the feels, dusted myself off, and got back to it.

Here are a few tips for staying present:

- Four corner breathing (deep breath in, hold for four seconds, slowly release breath over four seconds, wait four seconds, and repeat)
- Listen to an upbeat playlist—and move your body
- Read a book
- Play with a child (they're always so remarkably present)

Here's the bottom line: eventually something will disrupt your day-to-day activities as a business owner. Spending time *now* to put plans in place for when it does will help you through whatever challenges come your way. Rest, if you must, but don't you quit!

Key Takeaways

- Accept help when offered;
- Create a delegation plan;
- Set aside funds to cover three months of living and business expenses;
- Stay present; and
- Cultivate a positive mindset.

Entrepreneurship and Adversity Go Hand in Hand

Cathy Agasar

I WAS FORTUNATE TO HAVE WONDERFUL OPPORTUNITIES TO learn about business in high school and college through my active involvement in Future Business Leaders of America (FBLA). I knew from a young age I wanted to head up a company, even though there were few female executives at the time. I was always encouraged by my parents to reach for the stars, and my advisors and mentors encouraged me to keep moving forward toward my career goals.

It all served me well as I became an award-winning, certified, professional marketer, rising to the level of vice president of marketing for a regional bank. I even had a marketing consulting business with my husband, but after his sudden death, I eventually decided I didn't want to be in marketing anymore.

Reinventing myself didn't happen overnight. Through a series of events, like my children growing up and not needing me and the biggest realization that I needed to be around people, and I really wanted to work and be creative; however, I also knew I could never work for someone else again. With a "can do" attitude, I looked at business opportunities: making products seemed a little too much.;

property management might be interesting; or a franchise, maybe. And then I got an email.

The subject line read, "Lower Bucks Chamber Business for Sale." As an active chamber member, my reaction was, "Who's selling their business and why I don't know about it?" I opened the email only to find it was from a member broker listing all the businesses on the market. I scrolled through the listing, and one actually stood out: Newtown Day Spa. With input from my accountant, I decided to check it out; anything was possible, right?

I met with the broker and owner, and it was a good thing I didn't have my checkbook with me; I fell in love with the facility and the idea of owning a spa! Five and a half months later, I was the proud owner of a holistic wellness day spa—and I knew nothing about how to run it!

Let's back up a minute. During the due diligence period, I assembled an advisory team of people I trusted: my accountant, personal banker, insurance agent, attorney, graphic and web designer, marketing consultant, business coach, and a friend in a small business (fun fact: I still rely on the advice of six of these individuals after twelve years). Each brought knowledge and insights to the purchasing process for me. As we reviewed documents, made projections, and went back and forth with questions, I wondered about the viability of the signature service: colon hydrotherapy.

I'll never forget the day someone asked me how I was going to make money cleaning poop. *Cleaning poop.* Not understanding what colon hydrotherapy really was, the idea of "cleaning poop" didn't sound so fantastic.

My confident answer was, "If the previous owner could do it, I'm sure I can too." I knew about business operations and marketing, so how hard could it be to keep revenues coming in? But even as I sounded confident, I began to have second thoughts.

I'd come too far in this process to back out. My new game plan: phase out colon hydrotherapy after the sale was completed. That would solve my problems. Then, about two weeks before closing, a little voice told me I needed to learn more about colon hydrotherapy. And I didn't just want to learn the skill from the owner's perspective, I wanted to become certified so I could answer questions and have people take me seriously.

I do believe God led me to buy this particular business, even though at the time I had no idea what colonhydrotherapy was. I felt there was a beautiful plan for my life making that leap, but understanding evolved on the long journey.

The day after signing the papers, I began learning the business. Two things became very clear that first day: one, I needed to learn as much as I could about holistic living, and two, I needed to stop drinking soda, specifically Diet Coke. The first task seemed like fun, as I enjoyed learning something new; the second would be a challenge because I had grown up drinking soda and Diet Coke was my beverage of choice.

I believed I was fairly healthy when I bought the business, but learning about holistic health was an eye-opening experience. I stopped drinking Diet Coke cold turkey and spent the next year and a half detoxifying my body of its affects. I changed the way I shopped, the cleaning products I used, the skin care products I wore, and even the kind of water I drank. Yep, I had a lot to learn to be congruent with my business and the services we provided.

As I settled into daily business life and learned more about holistic living, I realized there really was a mind/body/spirit connection called "whole living." I could easily talk about wellness but knew if I truly wanted to make a difference for myself and others, I had to walk the talk. Living in alignment with my business wasn't taught to me—and this business was unlike any I'd previously encountered.

I settled into owning a holistic wellness day spa and did so pretty easily. My extensive customer service background helped with with meeting and dealing with clients. I took care of every aspect of business ownership: the banking, bookkeeping, client records, marketing, etc. The biggest eye-opener was dealing with employees. Sure, I had had employees in corporate, but I never had to deal with human resources. I had a huge learning curve with payroll, scheduling, policies and procedures, unemployment, and people not showing up for work...the list felt endless.

Running a business takes time, but it also has to be in balance with family life. Seven months after purchasing the spa, I returned from a trip to England to find that my oldest son had made some very poor choices, choices that continued for the next ten years. I scrambled to retain my sanity, as well as keeping my family together and the business moving forward. I felt like a piece of taffy, stretched in opposite directions, and caught in a vicious. Most days, I felt the walls closing in.

By my fifth business anniversary, my business (and I) was in trouble. Because of my son's challenges, I missed a lot of time. And, truth be told, I'd not taken my health seriously—it was difficult to focus on anything during this dark time.

That's when I hit a turning point.

Coming to understand when something had to give was truly life changing. I went back to learning, asking questions, and working on me to come through the second darkest time in my life. Do I wish I'd known more during those first few years? Yes, but I also know that experience was the best teacher and learning how to move forward in positive ways brought the most rewards.

Through my almost twelve years of spa ownership, I have learned invaluable lessons. I don't know if I would have embraced them all during that first year, but, looking back, I do believe doing so would have made a difference. I share these lessons with you:

- **Take time to breathe.** As someone who is driven, pausing was not part of my life. Learning to take time to breathe and just BE has had a powerful affect on my business.
- **Learn something new every day**. I loved learning new things, but when I finally set my mind to learn at least one thing each day, my world opened up; I've

become a better version of myself, and a better businesswoman.

- **Get up and move**. We live in a digital world and owning a business often requires long hours at the computer, which is draining and unhealthy. It's crucial to take a two-minute stretch break every hour. Who knows? It might just make the work easier to get done.

- **Surround yourself with talented people**. No woman is an island. Find the right people to assist you. Have a plan for how things will get done, and count on others to help achieve the plan. Just because you're a solopreneur doesn't mean you are the only one who can do something.

- **Be frictionless**. Develop your processes and make decisions that make sense for your business model. Keep things simple, focused, and profitable. Keep processes easy to manage and reduce the friction for you, your staff, and customers.

- **Drink more water**. Made you chuckle, right? That's what I thought when someone told me years ago, but when I actually started drinking more water, I felt better and had more energy to get through the day—a game changer in many ways.

- **Have an attitude of gratitude**. Nothing moves forward if you are not grateful. The first few years of business are challenging, so be grateful for what you have and what you are building.

- **Be open to possibilities**. I never thought I would date again, let alone fall in love, and get married a second time. When I opened myself to possibilities in my personal life, my business flourished too. I became attractive to the Universe, my new husband, and—most of all—myself. We merged two families, two homes, and two business for twice the fun! Funny how that works.

I THOUGHT I KNEW IT ALL WHEN I BOUGHT THE SPA, BUT I didn't. I still don't. I love what I have created, and that my growing passion for self-care has been a catalyst for many exciting opportunities. The adversity that led me to this point in my life was not easy, but learning lessons along the way, I now have a legacy of experiences to help others find their passions and dreams of business ownership. How awesome is that?

KEY TAKEAWAYS

- Develop your personal "board of directors" to guide, support, and encourage you as you build and grow your business.
- Believe in yourself and your skills, trusting that you can learn what you need along the way.
- Remain open and curious for what may come your way once you lean into yourself.
- Things that appear to be happening "to you" may actually be happening "for you."

About Our Authors

Cathy Agasar, author of *The Gift of Loss*, is a national board certified colon hydrotherapist and I-ACT certified colon hydrotherapy instructor. Her own wellness journey brought her to a new level of understanding of the mind/body/spirit connection and a passion to educate the public about gut health and cleansing. Cathy and her husband, Jerry, reside and work in historic Bucks County, Pennsylvania, where they have merged their practices to serve the community together. She is the mother of six children and two cats and enjoys taking long walks, biking, reading, but, most of all, spending time with loved ones. She is a woman of strong faith, grateful every day for the life she is living, and extremely honored to share her journey with all who will listen. Learn more at https://agasarfamilywellcare.com/.

Cheri D. Andrews, Esq., your small business attorney, helps women-owned small businesses ensure that their businesses are legally compliant and protected. Cheri is an award-winning attorney and bestselling author of *Smooth Sailing: A Practical Guide to Legally Protecting Your Business*. She received her Bachelor of Arts degree, magna cum laude, from Mount Holyoke College and her *Juris Doctor* degree from Temple University School of Law. Cheri has over thirty years' law firm and corporate experience. Her practice areas include business formation, contracts, policies, copyright, and trademark. Learn more at www.cheriandrews.com.

Gabriela Bocanete is an international conference interpreter, trainer, and speaker based near London, UK. She is also a holistic health coach and sound therapy practitioner. She draws on her multi-disciplinary knowledge and expert understanding of stress, its causes and consequences, to offer bespoke interventions that improve brain performance and resilience. Her clients call her live gong meditation sessions the BrainSpa. She is the creator of several online courses and a speaker at professional associations conferences. Learn more at [URL].

Hanne Brøter is a graphic designer, visual branding expert, and teacher of graphic design. Her passion is helping entrepreneurs create and maintain a visual look of their businesses that reflects their brand message in a unique and authentic way. She works with entrepreneurs through her business Your Brand Vision and through Broter School of Design, where she teaches graphic design to non-designers who wants to leverage the power of correct graphic design in their marketing. Learn more at www.YourBrandVision.com.

Jill Celeste, MA, loves Loud Women and loud bassets. That's why you will likely find her teaching marketing and mindset to female entrepreneurs at Celestial University; or facilitating sisterhood and connection through her online networking organization, Virtual Networkers; or hanging out with basset hounds as the co-founder of Tampa Bay Basset Hounds. She's the bestselling author of two books (so far): *Loud Woman* and *That First Client*. She lives near Tampa, Florida, with her husband, two sons, two cats, and a basset hound named Trixie. To learn more about Jill, please visit http://Jill Celeste.com.

In 2008, **Maureen "Mo" Cooper** was disappointed that her fourth and last child didn't weigh sixty pounds. Mo just felt like she did! At thirty-nine, Mo knew that enough was enough! She had never exercised, was living with Multiple Sclerosis, and a full-time mom;

"living" felt more like "surviving." She started making small changes: exercise replaced groggy mornings and packaged foods were swapped for fresh. Losing weight and feeling great became her passion. This personal trainer and nutrition coach lives her message of health by coaching clients to success with small, doable strategies. Learn more at www.momindbodysoul.com.

Maribeth Decker is bestselling author of *Peace of Passing: Comfort for Loving Humans During Animal Transitions* and the founder of SacredGrove.com—Where People and Pets Heal and Connect. She works with animal guardians who dearly love their animals and yet are facing tough animal issues. She uses her intuitive animal communication, medical intuition, and energetic healing skills to address animals' physical, emotional, and behavioral issues. Maribeth's mission is to bring a greater depth of love, compassion, and comfort into the human-animal relationship. Learn more at www.SacredGrove.com.

Jennifer Kate is a spiritual transformation coach and energy healer with over a decade of experience as a multi-passionate entrepreneur. Her coaching focuses on self-discovery, self-transformation, energy management, and uses her proprietary MAGIC framework to help clients make the profound shifts that they have longed to make in order to start living life on their own terms, a life by design. She holds undeniable gifts for discerning truth and pure intentions, and her ability to ask powerful intuitive questions, in a field of love, sets her apart in the world of transformational practitioners. Learn more at https://jenkate.com/.

Donna Kendrick is the author of *A Guide to Widowhood: Navigating the First Three Years* and owner of Sephton Financial where she works as a financial professional helping families in transition. Her practice was created as a result of her own journey into widowhood at the age of forty. Her practice was created for the person whose tomorrow is very different from their today, whether it be through widowhood, divorce, or a career change. Learn more at https://sephtonfinancial.com/.

Deborah Kevin (pronounced "KEY-vin"), MA, as the founder and chief inspiration officer of Highlander Press, loves helping change-makers tap into and share their stories of healing and truth with impactful books, including her book entitled *You've Written Your Book. Now What?* Debby, a graduate of Stanford University's Novel Writing program, earned a master's degree in publishing from Western Colorado University. She's trekked over 350 miles of the Camino de Santiago, and she lives in Maryland with the love of her life, Rob, her sons, and their puppy Fergus—that is when they're not off discovering the world.

Learn more at https://highlanderpressbooks.com.

Pam Knox is a global business consultant, communication coach, and strategic storyteller. She helps entrepreneurs and executives harness their thought leadership, build their brands, and reach revenue goals by aligning their business strategy with a well-executed people strategy. She is passionate about building a better world through better communication. Her business, Pam Knox LLC, equips business owners with the tools to confidently tell their business story, lead strategically, and engage audiences through shared thought leadership. Learn more at https://pamknox.com.

Nancy Linnerooth releases subconscious blocks holding women entrepreneurs back from the next level in their business using EFT (or "tapping"). She draws on nine years as a Harvard Law School-trained attorney, seventeen years as a therapist, and over fifteen years practicing EFT/Tapping. With straight talk and humor, Nancy helps clients release the causes of procrastination, self-sabotage, and Imposter Syndrome. With her help, clients finally follow through on their dreams and create the life they've always wanted. Learn more at https://unblockresults.com/.

Kelly Lutman is a certified health coach and best-selling author who uses functional medicine principles to help her clients reclaim their health by finding the root cause of their symptoms and dis-ease. Whether the issue is named IBS, diabetes, Hashimoto's, arthritis, or a host of other diagnosis, Kelly meets each client where they are and educates them on what's happening inside their bodies. Since each of our bodies is unique, she approached each client based on their individual needs, coming alongside them to guide them in nourishing their body as they pursue wellness. Learn more at www.PursueWellnessForYou.com.

Margaret Martin, author of *The Chatter that Matters – Your Words ARE Your Power* and *Your Chatter Matters – Journal of Gratitude*, lives in the Tampa Bay area. She works with women in her "Re-Design Your Life" program for women in their 50s, 60s, 70s to believe in themselves again one thought at a time so they can step into their power and do the work they were meant to do in this world. Learn more at www.MargaretMartin.com.

Nicole Meltzer, author of *Intuitive Languages* and founder of the transformative program Flow, has helped thousands of people tap into and trust their intuition through her international intuitive circles, programs, and presentations. Nicole's lust for travel, art, languages, and architecture have her seeking bridges—both physically and metaphorically—to connect with others. She lives with her soulmate of many lifetimes, Elliott, and their two highly intuitive sons in Newmarket, Ontario, Canada, where the artsy vibe blends with sporty spice. Learn more at https://www.balancedu.ca/.

Connie Jo Miller has loved numbers since first grade when her teacher used a plywood cut-out man with clothes pins for fingers to teach addition and subtraction. Connie Jo's first career was as a mechanical engineer in the corporate world (lots of numbers there). Next, she homeschooled her two kids from birth through high school. Sadly, math was neither kid's favorite subject. Now, Connie Jo is a bookkeeping professional and financial coach who still loves numbers, especially the ones with dollar signs in front of them! Learn more at https://www.enigmabookkeepingsolutions.com/.

Suzanne Tregenza Moore helps non-fiction authors focus on revenue and thought leadership status. Since leaving her six-figure job, Suzanne has employed her MBA in Marketing & Entrepreneurship, along with personal experience from living in the weeds of her business, to support clients with strategy, marketing, technology, delegation, and mindset. Clients describe her as "invaluable" and a "gentle butt-kicker." She is the best-selling author of *Hang on Tight! Learn to Love the Roller Coaster of Entrepreneurship*. Learn more at http://suzannetmoore.com.

Orianna Nienan is the Founder of Product Love, an eCommerce brand focused on supporting, promoting and developing attractive, eco-friendly products. Orianna's personal mission includes normalizing sustainable products, making them equally attractive to less environmentally responsible alternatives. Her focus is on influencing consumer demand to drive corporate change rather than advocating for increased environmental legislation. She loves contemplating what is possible and holding positive visions for the Earth's future. Visit www.product-love.com for more information about her brand.

Laura Templeton's heart physically hurt as she watched business owners and professionals in her network struggle to share their brilliance in thirty seconds or less. She had a simple formula that could help so she started teaching. As a global speaker and best-selling author of *30 Second Success: Ditch the pitch and start connecting!*, Laura inspires audiences and clients to dig deep and find the words that connect with the people they are meant to serve. For more information, visit https://30SecondSuccess.com.

Kate Varness, soul purpose + clarity coach, helps coaches and consultants to get paid for their brilliance because they embody their Human Design. Kate holds certifications in Quantum Human Design, professional organizing, and productivity coaching. She's happiest matching clients with marketing strategies that feel good and messaging that's simply irresistible. A multi-book author and international speaker, Kate lives in central Illinois with her husband, three kids, and Chief Operating Dog, Mickey. Learn more at Kate-Varness.com.

Straight-talking no-nonsense business coach, **Clare Whalley** runs Meta4 Business Coaching, and works with creative and ambitious business owners. Celebrating fifteen years in business, she guides businesses through structured coaching programs that share proven strategies to achieve more profitability and balance. Helping business owners navigate key business growth challenges from making more money without the chaos through to motivating and developing a team, for them to grow a business to be proud of, one that inspires and motivates so they can create more of what they love. Author of *Do.It.Now! A practical Workbook to Make your Business Work Harder, Not You.* Clare expresses apologies to her readers for the Queen's English being changed to the colonies' English. Learn more at https://meta4coaching.co.uk/.

Lee Murphy Wolf, creator of The Calibrate Method™, is on a mission to help female entrepreneurs trust their inner wisdom. She teaches her clients how to translate the language of their souls, make aligned choices, and master their personal energy, so they can step into their next level of business growth with clarity and confidence. Learn more about her services at www.LeeMurphyWolf.com.

Copyright Information

About the Publisher

Highlander Press, founded in 2019, is a mid-sized publishing company committed to diversity and sharing big ideas thereby changing the world through words.

Highlander Press guides authors from where they are in the writing-editing-publishing process to where they have an impactful book of which they are proud, making a long-time dream come true. Having authored a book improves your confidence, helps create clarity, and ensures that you claim your expertise.

What makes Highlander Press unique is that their business model focuses on building strong collaborative relationships with other women-owned businesses, which specialize in some aspect of the publishing industry, such as graphic design, book marketing, book launching, copyrights, and publicity. The mantra "a rising tide lifts all boats" is one they embrace.

facebook.com/highlanderpress

instagram.com/highlanderpress

linkedin.com/highlanderpress

pinterest.com/highlanderpress

Made in United States
Orlando, FL
08 March 2023

30839821R00102